To the Promised Land

To the

THE · BIRTH

Promised Land

OF · ISRAEL

Uri Dan

Doubleday
NEW YORK LONDON TORONTO SYDNEY

Published by Doubleday, a division of Bantam Doubleday Dell
Publishing Group, Inc., 666 Fifth Avenue, New York, N.Y. 10103

DOUBLEDAY and the portrayal of an anchor with a dolphin are
trademarks of Doubleday, a division of Bantam Doubleday Dell
Publishing Group, Inc.

Library of Congress Cataloging-in-Publication Data

Dan, Uri.
    To the Promised Land

    Translation of: Exodus et la Naissance d'Israël
    1. Israel—History—1948–1949. 2. Zionism—History
I. Harel, Yossi. II. Title
DS126.5.D2414   1988   956.94′052   87-37528
ISBN 0-385-24597-1

Photo credits appear on page 285.
Originally published in France as *Exodus et la Naissance d'Israël*
    by Uri Dan, Yossi Harel
Copyright © 1987 by Fixot
Translation copyright © 1988 by Uri Dan

KP

FOREWORD

The Year 2000 in Jerusalem

THE ESTABLISHMENT of the state of Israel is by far the greatest event in the history of the Jewish people in the last two thousand years and one of the most significant events of the twentieth century. Forty years have passed since Israel declared its independence and determined to fight for it. When I look back on the colossal hurdles and obstacles that the Jews in Israel have surmounted to build their country and ensure its security, my optimism is only reinforced. We are now moving toward the year 2000 in a Jerusalem of peace.

For two thousand years the Jews dreamed and struggled in order to realize their fervent prayer in their lands of dispersion: "Next year in Jerusalem"—Jerusalem, the capital city of the Jewish people for over three thousand years, since the days of King David. And they have in fact returned to Jerusalem. They can

today say with a measure of certainty and with a great deal of faith, "We will have a peace parade in Jerusalem in the year 2000: a parade of Israeli achievements in the fields of medicine and music, science and agriculture, in all walks of life in which Jews have been the standard-bearers since the dawn of history." I believe that there will also be a parade of peace in Jerusalem, peace between Israel and its Arab neighbors.

My belief that we will indeed make peace with the Arabs does not stem from wishful thinking. For most of my life I have fought that cruel Palestinian terror which has tried unsuccessfully to uproot us from Eretz Yisrael. It has been my lot to take part in all of the military campaigns in the defense of Israel against Arab armies. I have known great moments of victory, just as I have experienced the most terrible moments on battlefields swept

The young sublieutenant Ariel Sharon at the head of his company, January 1948.

by deadly fire. Only someone who was there and took part in those wars is truly able to appreciate peace.

That is why Israel wants peace: because, over the last forty years, we have been on the battlefield incessantly—from the War of Independence in 1948, to the expulsion of Yasir Arafat's PLO from Beirut in August 1982, and the bombing of PLO headquarters in Tunis in October 1985, as well as in the daily struggle against terror. But we do not seek a peace of Munich: not a peace of surrender and of future dangers but, rather, a peace between equals. The Arabs will reconcile themselves to this only if Israel is strong. The late President of Egypt, Anwar al-Sadat, understood this and came to Jerusalem in November 1977 to negotiate a peace treaty with Israel after nearly thirty years of conflict.

I look forward to Israel's future with optimism and back on its past without nostalgia. I do so first and foremost because of my knowledge of the spirit of the Jewish people. My brethren do not despair in the most critical of moments. The very opposite: It is then, when things look absolutely bleak and hopeless, that they arise to perform the most astonishing feats.

Some of the world's top military experts predicted that the State of Israel, which had then just come into being, could not survive against the seven Arab armies that invaded it on May 15, 1948. Yet the war ended with an Arab defeat, save in the Gaza Strip, which was captured by the Egyptians, and the West Bank, which remained under Jordanian occupation. In June 1967 many people both in and out of Israel feared for the country's fate when Egyptian, Syrian, Iraqi, and Jordanian forces massed on its borders. The Six-Day War ended with the capture of Sinai, the Gaza Strip, the Golan Heights, Judea, and Samaria. Most important of all, the Old City of Jerusalem was liberated and Israel's capital united once more. In October 1973 Egypt and Syria surprised Israel, but the war ended with our crossing the Suez Canal and threatening Cairo. When PLO terrorists hijacked a plane with many Israeli passengers to Entebbe Airport in Uganda, Israeli troops freed them in a breathtaking operation as the United States celebrated the bicentennial of liberty on July 4, 1976. And when Iraq threatened to produce nuclear arms aimed at Israel, we destroyed its atomic reactor near Baghdad in a unique air raid on June 7, 1981.

It is the spirit of the Israelis that has made success possible in all these operations: a spirit they have translated into richly imaginative action and great deeds of bravery, but principally into dogged determination and the preparedness for self-sacrifice to an extent that is hard to conceive. It is a spirit that derives from the unassailable belief that we have full right to Eretz Yisrael.

This spirit has been and remains Israel's most powerful weapon. It has pervaded every act of the Israeli people throughout the present period of our history, a chapter that began more than one hundred years ago, when Jews started returning en masse to their homeland.

Many are unaware that the Jews maintained a continuous presence in Eretz Yisrael even as the bulk of Jewry was dispersed to the four corners of the earth. At no time did Jewish settlement in the country cease, even during the darkest days of repressive Muslim, Crusader, and Ottoman rule. Jews in the thousands always held on, in the most difficult circumstances, to pray at Jerusalem's Western Wall; they sank their roots into the stones of Hebron and Safad and the basalt rocks of Tiberias.

But when persecution of the Jews intensified, the political Zionist movement was born. With the changes that took place in the Middle East after World War I, the return of the Jews to their country gained tremendous momentum. For the first time in history a nation was reborn after two thousand years of forced banishment.

Never were the Jews bothered by the fact that they were a minority in Eretz Yisrael, surrounded by millions of Muslims in neighboring Arab countries. They were always a people small in number, and Eretz Yisrael has forever been a tiny strip of land compared to the expansive tracts in Arab countries.

The slaughter of one third of the Jewish people by the Nazis in World War II was the greatest disaster that has befallen the nation since its exile from its homeland. The enormous dimensions of the Holocaust served to strengthen the belief that we were obligated to bring the survivors to Eretz Yisrael in whatever ways were possible, and our safety and peace could never be assured until we were masters of our own destiny.

From the start, the Jewish people's struggle for their own state has been based on three closely related paths that unite into one. They are as relevant today as ever: uninterrupted Jewish immigration, settling the land in every possible location, and the setting up of a people's army. The State of Israel was established to ensure for Jews independent boundaries, just like those of other nations. The settlements in Galilee and the Negev, in Judea and Samaria and the Jordan Valley, became the most effective means of returning to the land for a nation accustomed to wandering for thousands of years. Jews also learned that they were obliged to protect these settlements with their own weapons and their own efforts.

Ariel Sharon, the present Israeli Minister for Industry and Commerce, during the 1960s.

They had no one else to rely on. The settlements have become an integral part of Israel's defensive mechanism for blunting and containing the enemy attack until such time as the people's army, the reserve deployment, can be called up.

On November 29, 1947, the General Assembly of the United Nations passed a resolution establishing a Jewish state in Eretz Yisrael. But that resolution would have remained on paper, suffering the same fate as countless other U.N. resolutions passed since then, had the Jews not been prepared to stand up and fight.

One can accurately describe Zionism as one of the most successful and positive revolutionary movements in modern world history. Contrary to many other so-called freedom-fighter movements, which sow random terror and cause death to innocent victims, the aim of the Zionist revolution is construction, not destruction. Militarism in itself, wars and campaigns —however brilliant they may be—are valueless if they are not designed to defend the existence, development, and safety of society and the state. I say this as one who knows the battlefield all too well from more than thirty years as a soldier, and as one who has served as a minister in Israeli governments for the last ten years. Were the sum total of Israel's history confined to great deeds of war, I would view this as an abject failure of the Zionist revolution. But we succeeded, during and between the wars imposed on us, in building hundreds of settlements and towns and absorbing millions of immigrants from 102 countries, who spoke 82 different languages yet who learned Hebrew here. Because we succeeded in developing an amazing agriculture, in building a sophisticated and advanced industrial infrastructure, and in setting up outstanding and progressive scientific institutions and universities to educate generations to come who will continue the struggle, and because we made Jerusalem an important center of the world, there is some compensation for the amount of blood and sweat that the soil of Eretz Yisrael has absorbed. The Zionist revolution has accomplishments of which very few revolutionary movements can boast.

This revolution is only in its infancy. Our War of Independence ended in 1949, but our fight for liberation continues to this day. The Middle East is a region that, down through the ages, has lent itself to trouble and strife. To deter the Arabs from waging war and bring them to the negotiating tables to talk peace, we must ensure the existence and survival of these three paths of Zionism. Since by our nature we are a nation of revolutionaries, I believe that the Zionist movement will produce new ideas and means to strengthen Israel. Every revolution has its ups and downs. Every revolution needs stimulating injections of what may be termed "a revolution within a revolution."

In this struggle, as always, all Jews are partners. The State of Israel must be regarded as a joint venture of the Jews in Israel and those outside it. If the Jewish people can be considered a body, then the State of Israel is its heart. The organism cannot survive without a healthy heart in a muscular body, a body hardened by fire and sword, by suffering and struggle and building and developing. There are still in that body great forces that have not been unleashed, forces capable of turning Israel into a world center in many creative fields, a center that can contribute much to the world in general, and to our Arab neighbors in the Middle East in particular.

The foundation for peace between us and the Palestinians has been laid, notwithstanding the serious difficulties and enormous obstacles that still lie before us. Perseverance and patience will help Israel build a bridge of peace over the Jordan River between Israel and the Palestinian state, between Jerusalem and Amman. Across that bridge a new and young Israeli generation, one which I know so well, and which surpasses all the generations that preceded it, will stride in peace when the time comes.

Ariel Sharon

May 15, 1948

*The Final Hour:
on May 14, 1948, the British
lower their flag and leave
Palestine.*

MOST ISRAELIS remember Saturday, May 15, 1948, as the first free day of the reborn Jewish state in Eretz Yisrael.* I remember it as the day the Egyptian Air Force bombed my Bar Mitzvah. That is my vivid memory of the first day of the reborn Jewish state, the first hours of its War of Independence. This was the first of the wars between Israel and the regular armies of its Arab neighbors—all of these having taken place in the forty years following independence.

For more than six months Palestine had been awash in blood. On Friday afternoon, May 14, David Ben-Gurion, leader of the Palestinian Jewish community, proclaimed the establishment of the State of Israel in a short but emotional ceremony in the Tel Aviv Museum. At that moment he became the country's acting Prime Minister, serving also as Minister of Defense, a post he continued to fill, with short intervals, for some fifteen years. Ben-Gurion originally thought of calling the state Judea, after the Jewish kingdom that had been destroyed. However, nearly two thousand years ago preference had eventually been given to the name Israel, which is the name

that God, according to the biblical story, gave Jacob, one of the founding fathers of the Hebrew people. According to the Bible, Jacob wrestled with an angel, a messenger of the Lord, and defeated him. Israel—that was God's name for someone who could overcome an angel. But this newborn Israel would be called upon to fight a devil, the demon of war.

The first kingdom of Israel was ruled by King Saul, expanded under David, and prospered in the reign of King Solomon, during about 1030–933 B.C. The ancient Jewish nation was then split into two: the kingdom of Judea and the kingdom of Israel. Yet the people in both kingdoms were known by one name, the people of Israel. They were called by that name by the great prophets who arose among them. The name Jew comes from the kingdom of Judea. Since the people of Israel were also those who ruled in the kingdom of Judea, the name Jew became synonymous with the name Israeli.

Ben-Gurion decided that the new state would be called Israel, that is, "the Jewish State." In his eyes, Israel and Jews were on an equal footing. "We hereby proclaim the establishment of the Jewish state in Eretz Yisrael. It is the State of Israel," Ben-Gurion proclaimed on May 14, 1948. If many Jews regarded Ben-Gurion as a new Jewish king, a successor to David and Solomon, he saw himself rather as a prophet with a clear socialist outlook, a prophet who fate had decreed would command the most crucial campaign in his people's deliverance, not merely a philosophical sage. I heard Ben-Gurion's voice on

* The Holy Land or Promised Land, as most of the world referred to it, was always known to the Jews as Eretz Yisrael, "the land of Israel." It included the territories of ancient Israel, promised in the Bible to the Jews by God, including the kingdoms of David and Solomon. The original Palestine Mandate on both sides of the Jordan River—most of which was detached by the British to create an Arab state known today as the Hashemite Kingdom of Jordan—included all of the territory of Eretz Yisrael. Before statehood, the Jews used "Eretz Yisrael" to refer to the entire biblical land of Israel; since then, most Jews use the term to mean the current boundaries of the State of Israel.

On May 14, 1948, David Ben-Gurion, standing beneath a portrait of Theodor Herzl, proclaims the creation of the State of Israel.

On May 15, 1948, the first Egyptian warplane is shot down over Tel Aviv during the War of Independence.

pose curfews in Tel Aviv to search for arms. We had a state.

At that tender age I could not absorb the full significance of the fact that, even at that very time, seven Arab armies were already marching into Eretz Yisrael, confident they would strangle the state in its infancy and uproot its citizens before they could become solidly rooted. I did not, at the moment, comprehend the real meaning of this. The Arab states—Egypt, Jordan, Syria, Iraq, Saudi Arabia, Yemen, and Lebanon—had decided to liquidate the Jewish state.

May 15, 1948, was therefore a double celebration for me. It was my thirteenth birthday —a special day in the life of every Jewish boy, a day on which he takes on the onus of carrying out the mitzvoth (commandments). I was a young citizen in my own country, a wonderful gift for a personal day of celebration. Since then my fate has been irrevocably linked with that of Israel, as has been true for so many others who were born in Israel or who immigrated there. I have always believed that every Israeli, even if just a bystander, shares the heavy burden of building the new state.

On that same Saturday, in accordance with Jewish custom, I went to the synagogue near my home in Tel Aviv to read the Torah, a portion of the Law. Tears of joy welled up in my parents' eyes. My father had received special furlough from the Haganah, the Jewish defense organization that was the forerunner of the Israeli Army. He had had to leave his post at the edge of Jaffa, the Arab town contiguous with Tel Aviv, where he and his colleagues defended us against snipers.

As we left the synagogue, the wail of air-raid sirens was heard in Tel Aviv, announcing oncoming enemy aircraft. The dull thuds of bombs could be heard, and palls of smoke rose above the city's low-rise houses. Tel Aviv was being bombed for the first time by the Egyptian Air Force.

The tables at our house were laden with all

the radio that Friday, and it was the clear and decisive voice of a leader. A quiver of excitement ran through me. "We have our own state!" I realized. As a boy of thirteen born in Tel Aviv, I knew this had only one meaning: The hated British would no longer rule over us. No more would they hang our boys who had fought them. No longer would they im-

16

sorts of fruit, cakes, and drinks, but most of the guests never arrived. People chose not to leave their homes, preferring to be close to air-raid shelters. My parents tried to comfort me. But I remember telling them, "There's nothing to be sorry about. I received a fantastic present: the state."

This small personal cameo of a young boy witnessing such great drama symbolizes to some extent all I have seen and experienced in the State of Israel in these last forty years. This is a state in which there is no joy without blood. There has not been a moment's peace in the Promised Land. We have known both the exultation of triumph and the gloomy silence of the cemetery. Along the way we have lost some of our best friends. All too often we have heard the volleys of last salvos over coffins being lowered at military funerals.

Zubin Mehta, the renowned conductor, once told me that each time he conducts the Israel Philharmonic he reflects with infinite sadness on the number of great musicians the world lost when Hitler exterminated millions of Jews. I replied that among the thousands of Israelis who have met their death on the battlefield there were also many with outstanding musical talent. As with the six million, there were also great geniuses in science and medicine, mathematics and literature—all those fields in which the Jewish people have been at the forefront. In Israel's wars, the cream of our youth had fallen, because it was always they who went first, as commanders and as soldiers.

Since 1948 I have witnessed each of Israel's wars, from the Suez Campaign in 1956, through the War of Attrition along the Suez Canal in 1969–70, and up to the 1982 war in Lebanon against local, regional, and international terror and the expulsion of Yasir Arafat's PLO. In 1956 I jumped with the first Israeli paratroopers—Battalion 890—into the Mitla Pass. In 1973 I was on one of the first armored personnel carriers to cross the Suez

Embarkation of the last British troops in Palestine at Haifa, May 1948.

Canal. During the war in Lebanon I served as media adviser to the Minister of Defense. In the intervening years it has been my privilege to follow those who were Israel's leaders and commanders during the War of Independence and get to know most of them up close.

Forty years is an exceedingly short time in the life of a nation, especially one whose history dates back 3,700 years. The nation that gave the world the Bible, itself a unique history book, should ask whether these forty years are worthy of being recorded as one more page in the book that tells about the Exodus from Egypt, the wandering in Sinai for forty years before entering the land of Canaan, the Kingdom of David, and Solomon's Temple in Jerusalem.

For forty years Moses led his people in the wilderness before God allowed him to bring this flock of Hebrew slaves who had left Egypt to the gates of the land of Canaan and wrest it from heathen idolaters. This period of wandering was punishment for having made and worshipped a golden calf while Moses ascended Mount Sinai to bring back the two tablets of the Ten Commandments that spelled out universal precepts and codes of conduct. Only after the wilderness generation had died out were its children divided into twelve tribes and allowed to enter the land of Canaan—on both sides of the Jordan River.

The first forty years in the history of modern Israel bear some resemblance to the wandering in the wilderness. Once again the Jewish nation had to be reestablished in its own land. But this time, instead of only 12 tribes entering the Promised Land, there were 120 tribes, because during the two thousand years of exile the Jews were dispersed to every corner of the globe—from Georgia in Soviet Russia to Harbin in China, from Sa'na in the Yemen to Warsaw in Poland, from Ethiopia in Africa to remote villages of Romania, from the Casbah of Algiers to Brooklyn, New York.

Yet the moment the State of Israel was proclaimed, its gates were opened to every Jew wishing to return. Ben-Gurion became a modern Moses presiding over all the Jewish tribes. It was Ben-Gurion who in the Declaration of Independence defined Israel as the Jewish state. Any Jew desiring to immigrate to Israel might do so, immediately becoming a citizen of the state. That is what Ben-Gurion laid down.

Israel's own raison d'être is embodied in that resolution known as the Law of Return. The young state, without means or resources, opened its gates to hundreds of thousands of Jews from around the world who hurried back to it during its first years. The establishment of the Jewish state fired the imagination and the hopes of Jews all over the world. Jews arrived penniless from Europe. In Iraq and Egypt, where Jews were *dhimmi*, second-class citizens, the war with Eretz Yisrael only worsened their plight, and the pogroms perpetrated on them increased in fury. Hundreds of thousands of Jews from Baghdad and Cairo abandoned their belongings, accumulated over hundreds of years, and fled to Israel clutching sparsely filled suitcases.

The modern exodus of Jews from the lands of their exile to the State of Israel took on an exceptional impetus and momentum in world history.

The spirit of the ship *Exodus,* which became the symbol of the unflagging Jewish struggle against the British Empire, pervaded every move of the young state, which was compelled to fight on a number of fronts. Israel was obliged to absorb hundreds of thousands of Jewish refugees to increase its own forces against the enemies encircling it. But in spite of the poorly equipped force at its disposal, Israel thwarted and checked the Arab armies and emerged victorious over them.

Only the unique spirit of this people's great determination and belief in the justice of their cause, and their willingness to sacrifice, could have spurred the Jews to continue their struggle in Eretz Yisrael against incomprehensible odds, against the confident predictions of some of the world's greatest experts.

As a young boy in Tel Aviv, I heard the devastating news from Jerusalem that the Jewish Quarter had fallen to the Arab Legion following the equally tragic loss of Gush Etzion, a group of four Jewish kibbutzim not far from Jerusalem.

But there was never any panic in Tel Aviv. There was a feeling of confidence, a totally illogical feeling that, at the end of it all, we would defeat the Arabs. There was a spirit of assurance that the Jews would eventually surmount all obstacles and win the war. We youngsters were jealous of the older people—some not all that much older—who went out to fight in Tel Aviv, Jerusalem, and Galilee.

The importance of this unique spirit was highlighted by Ben-Gurion in a speech on June 19, 1948. At the height of the war he termed this spirit "Israel's secret weapon." He wished to say ". . . something about the army in general. Great things have been done in this field, but we are still a long way from the final goal. Let us not underestimate the

Jerusalem, May 1948: as the British leave police headquarters, the Israeli flag is hoisted above the city.

enemy forces—not just their numbers and their heavy equipment, but also their fighting ability. . . . These are regular, trained, and disciplined armies that do not fall short of the spirit and bravery of our own men. They know how to fight and they fight bravely. Our boys who have come into combat with them in the south and in the Latrun front have learned to respect them as soldiers. We have to make great efforts in many spheres so as not to fall short of them in belief and in discipline (I regret to say that in this respect not everything on our side is in order), and, to the greatest extent possible, in respect of equipment too.

"We have one secret weapon . . . which is perhaps the greatest of all and which promises chances of victory. It is incumbent on us to forge this weapon. This secret weapon is in your hands—in the hands of those who are present here and in the hands of those who are not here: the spirit that will eventually decide the battle in which we are involved. I say this after dealing for two years only with the matter of guns, machine guns and cannons and battleships and airplanes. I know the value of these things, which have fulfilled and will continue to fulfill no small role. The history of the equipping of our army is a fantastic story in itself and will go down as the most decisive factor in the history of this campaign. . . .

"But this spirit will be the decisive factor. Not this alone, however. Without faith and without discipline and without the armed forces and without equipment, artillery, and planes, this spirit alone will not be enough."

This spirit remains Israel's secret weapon today.

The Birth of Israel

The Underground

THAT, ON MAY 14, 1948, David Ben-Gurion was in a position to proclaim the State of Israel was because the Yishuv—the Jewish community of Palestine—had completed a working plan for independence.* Between 1945 and 1948 the Jews mobilized their strength both to bring about the withdrawal of the British and to prepare themselves for a possible war against the Arabs.

In the decisive phase of this struggle, a small cluster of Jews, numbering barely half a million in 1945, drew their moral strength from the greatest catastrophe in their history. The Holocaust did not sink the Jews of Palestine into the depths of despair; on the contrary, as news of the death camps filtered through, so with it grew their determination to bring the survivors to the land of Israel. And the more they came to learn the horrendous details of the Final Solution devised by the two mad Adolfs—Hitler and Eichmann —the stronger became their dream of a Jewish state, so that the Jews would be able to defend themselves against any repetition of that horror.

In Palestine the British authorities were confronted by three underground groups, all of which already had a certain amount of combat experience. The most important of these was the Haganah (Hebrew for "Defense"), whose roots date back to 1920, when the Jews had to defend themselves against Arab riots in Jerusalem. Realizing that the British Army was unable—or unwilling—to defend them from these attacks, the Jews formed a local self-defense force and armed it with revolvers and rifles, all carefully concealed from the British. Over the years a national headquarters was established to plan the defense of each area of the state.

In the spring of 1931, following Arab pogroms against the Jews of Hebron, Safad, and Jerusalem, Irgun Zvai Leumi (National Military Organization)—commonly called Etzel, from its initials, or the Irgun—was born. Its founders, most of whom lived in Jerusalem, were Haganah dissidents who had

---

* From the end of the nineteenth century, with the new surge in Jewish settlement there, the Jewish community of Eretz Yisrael became known before statehood as the Yishuv, from the Hebrew word for "settling."

23

accused the Haganah of incompetence during the attacks.

At that time there was still little thought of an armed struggle against the British Empire; yet for the members of the Irgun it was no longer enough simply to "defend" the Jews against Arab attacks—retaliatory attacks had to be organized. Because the leadership of the Haganah was controlled by the Socialist-oriented Labor parties, then the most powerful in the Yishuv, the dissident Irgun became tagged with a right-wing label.

When, in 1939, it became obvious upon publication of a British Colonial Department White Paper (position paper) that the British, despite their political commitment to a Jewish homeland in Palestine, were intent instead on establishing an Arab state with a small Jewish minority, attacks were launched directly against the Mandatory administration. These attacks represented the first such operations for the Irgun. Its fighters burned government offices and sabotaged telephone lines and railroad tracks.

The political leader of the Irgun, Vladimir Zev Jabotinsky, who also headed the anti-Socialist Revisionist wing of Zionism, called on his partisans to prepare themselves for "armed struggle" against the British. Up to that time the Russian-born Jabotinsky had been pro-British, trusting London's promise in the Balfour Declaration. When World War II broke out, the leaders of both the Haganah and Irgun, aware that the British and the Jews shared a common enemy, declared a truce in their struggle against the British; indeed, they actively participated in the fight against the Third Reich.

"We shall fight the war as if there were no White Paper," declared Ben-Gurion. "And

Menachem Begin, disguised as a rabbi to escape from the British, with his wife and son.

Moshe Dayan (left) at the end of the 1930s.

we shall fight the White Paper as if there were no war."

(In sharp contrast, Haj Amin al-Husseini, the Mufti of Jerusalem and spiritual leader of Arab Palestine, actively supported Hitler and moved to Berlin, where he played a key role in stopping efforts that would have saved some Jewish children from the gas chambers. Moreover, an Arab military unit joined forces with the army of the Reich.)

This decision was the principal reason for the birth of Lohamei Herut Yisrael (Freedom Fighters of Israel), also known, from its initials, as the Lehi, which was the smallest and most extreme of the Jewish underground groups. Its founder, Avraham Stern (Yair), after whom it became known as the Stern Group, was a brilliant ideologist as well as a moody poet. As second in command of the Irgun, he had demanded that anti-British attacks continue. Faced with his comrades' refusal, he left the Irgun in the summer of 1940 and formed his own resistance group. Two years later he was killed by the British, who had tracked him down.

Ben-Gurion and the Yishuv leaders actively pressured the British to create a special Jewish brigade to fight the Germans. In addition, in

25

Patrol in Kibbutz Ramat David, December 1938.

Yitzhak Sadeh, founder of the Palmach, in 1948.

1942 the Palmach (the name is an abbreviation of the Hebrew term Peluggot Machatz, or "shock troops"), destined to become the elite efficient fighting force of the Haganah, was created to resist the German advance toward Palestine through Benghazi and Tobruk.

The commander of its A Company was the young Yigal Allon; of B Company, Moshe Dayan. The Palmach also set up a German Unit, whose fighters—young, blue-eyed, and fair-haired—carried out commando operations behind enemy lines.

The Polish-born founder of Palmach, Yitzhak Sadeh, believed a people's army had to be prepared to carry out the most daring commando operations. Under his command, his young male and female volunteers divided their time between kibbutz work and military training. A spirit of comradeship reigned in the Palmach; officers did not wear their insignia of rank, and the units looked more like revolutionary communes.

Meanwhile, the fighters of the Haganah and Irgun took part in special commando operations together with the British intelligence service. So close was their cooperation that David Raziel, the brilliant young leader of the Irgun, was killed in May 1941, while on a British commando raid in Iraq. Haganah fighters were parachuted into Europe to try to save British and Jewish prisoners.

The Haganah in particular benefited from this collaboration. The Palestinian Jews who joined the British Army acquired valuable military experience—and were also able to steal weapons that greatly expanded the secret arsenal of the Haganah. But most Zionist leaders hoped that after the war Britain woiuld take into account that the Jews had been by their side, while the Arabs had aided the Germans.

On December 1, 1943, Menachem Begin was named to succeed Raziel as head of the Irgun. He was but thirty years old and had arrived in Palestine in a Polish Army uniform only the previous year, having already served a term in a Soviet forced-labor camp for his Zionist activity. In contrast to the charismatic Ben-Gurion, already an established leader of Labor Zionism, few in the Yishuv knew Begin, who hid in a cloak of secrecy. Yitzhak Shamir, the officer in charge of Stern Group operations, was even less well known.

Three months after assuming the leader-

Patrolling sentries in Kibbutz Allonim, December 1938.

Yitzhak Sadeh (in shorts) with Moshe Dayan (left) and Yigal Allon.

Yitzhak Shamir, leader of the Stern Group.

David Ben-Gurion with his wife, Paula.

ship of the Irgun, Begin proclaimed a rebellion against British power in Palestine. More than a year before the surrender of Berlin he foresaw the Allied victory and became convinced there was no chance a postwar Britain would accept a Jewish state in Palestine. The only solution, he believed, was to liberate Eretz Yisrael by armed struggle. But as long as the battle against Nazi Germany was being waged, he gave strict orders that no British military installations be attacked and no individual acts of terrorism be committed.

For Shamir and his Sternist colleagues, however, the only good Englishman was a dead Englishman. Any Briton in Palestine was a target, they declared, especially soldiers, policemen, and officers.

When London still refused to open the gates of Palestine to Jews even after news of Nazi atrocities reached the Allies, the Stern Group decided to assassinate Lord Moyne, the British Minister for Middle East Affairs, stationed in Cairo. On November 6, 1944, Moyne was cut down at point-blank range by two young Jews, Eliyahu Beit-Tzuri and Eliyahu Hakim. They escaped on a motorcycle but were later caught, condemned to death, and hanged.

The murder of Lord Moyne led to a near-fratricidal war within the Yishuv. Ben-Gurion and the leaders of the Yishuv condemned the Irgun and Lehi as terrorists; for six months, until June 1945, they ordered the Haganah to help the British hunt down the two groups' fighters in an operation known as "the Season." The Irgun suffered a heavy blow; the Stern Group was practically destroyed. Their members burned with the desire to launch retaliatory raids against the Haganah and Palmach, but Begin sent out an urgent message: "There will be no civil war."

Nevertheless, the hatred between the two factions of the Yishuv seethed openly; many feared the split would doom the Zionist movement. For the Labor Socialists who controlled the Jewish Agency,† Haganah, and Palmach open war against the British—with whom they hoped to curry favor for a political solution—was an invitation to suicide.

The Jewish Agency was also convinced that the Jews could never hope to oust the British from Palestine by military might. London controlled the postwar Middle East through Egypt, Transjordan, and Iraq. British intelligence was considered the best in the world, and its secret service in Palestine had made important inroads in the Jewish underground.

† The Jewish Agency was created as the overall coordinating central body of the Zionist movement, both inside and outside of Palestine. Its executive committee eventually became the first government of the Jewish state.

A "wanted list" issued by the British in 1945–46; top left, Menachem Begin.

The vow of the Haganah, Irgun, and the Stern Group—"We will chase the British out of Eretz Yisrael"—seemed to many a hollow slogan at best, an insane scream at worst.

The First Zionist

THREE TIMES A DAY, observant Jews have recited the prayer "To Jerusalem, Your city, we shall return, and dwell in her midst as You have promised." But, ironically, it was an assimilated journalist from Budapest who gave life to the eternal Jewish dream—unrealized since the destruction of Jerusalem and the Holy Temple by the Roman Empire in the year 70 —to rebuild a Jewish state in the land of the Bible.

As the Paris correspondent for a Viennese newspaper, Theodor Herzl was shaken by the anti-Jewish demonstrations that took place in Paris during the Dreyfus Affair, culminating on January 5, 1895, with the public degradation of the Jewish army captain who defiantly clung to his claim of innocence to a charge of treason.

One year later, on February 14, 1896, Herzl published a book called *Der Judenstaat (The Jewish State),* in which he affirmed with amazing foresight that his political vision of a Jewish homeland was both necessary and feasible.

According to Herzl, it was up to the Jews to keep his historical essay from turning into fiction. "If this generation is not capable of doing it," he wrote, "then another shall follow in its footsteps, better and more noble. Those Jews who wish it will restore their state and be worthy of it.

"Palestine is the land of our ancestors; the land which we have never forgotten, whose memory touches the heart of our people, whose name will rally our masses. We will be the honor guard of the holy places and our existence shall guarantee that our obligations are respected. This honor guard shall be the majestic symbol of the solution of the Jewish problem after the sufferings we have endured for eighteen hundred years."

In 1897 he organized an international Zionist conference in Basel, Switzerland. He would say later: "Fifty years from now it will be said that in Basel I founded the Jewish

Theodor Herzl, (1860–1904) founder of political Zionism.

British troops in the Old City of Jerusalem during the bitter fighting in October 1938.

state." His prediction was only a few months off the mark. And in June 1967 the Jews of Israel became the guardians of a united Jerusalem and the holy places of Judaism, Christianity, and Islam.

Herzl's political Zionism was to capture the imagination of the Jewish world, particularly after the bloody pogroms by Russian Cossacks in Kishinev in 1903, but he would not live to see its fulfillment; in July 1904 he died of a long-standing heart condition aggravated by exhaustion. He was only forty-four years old.

At the time of Herzl's death, Palestine was still part of the Ottoman Empire, which was then destroyed in the First World War. On December 11, 1917, with British troops having ousted the Turks from Palestine, Britain's General Edmund Allenby triumphantly took formal possession of Jerusalem.

One month earlier, Herzl's successors, led by Chaim Weizmann, had won from London the critical document known as the Balfour Declaration. On November 2, Arthur Balfour, the Foreign Secretary, released an official declaration—clearly intended to win reluctant Jewish support for U.S. entry into the war—committing the British to a Jewish state:

"His Majesty's government view with favour the establishment in Palestine of a national home for the Jewish people, and will use their best endeavours to facilitate the achievement of this object, it being clearly understood that nothing shall be done which may prejudice the civil and religious rights of existing non-Jewish communities in Palestine, or the rights and political status enjoyed by Jews in any other country."

On April 24, 1920, the San Remo Conference handed Great Britain the League of Na-

Scottish soldiers guarding the Citadel in Jerusalem in 1936.

A British patrol.

tions Mandate over Palestine. The Arabs, fearing the British would strip them of their rights, pressured London to slowly distance itself from the Balfour Declaration, and Palestine's 80,000 Jews began organizing for a long struggle.

33

Settling the Country

*Kibbutz Urim in the
Negev in 1947.*

IN 1909 Jewish settlers in Jaffa moved to the north of the city and established Tel Aviv, the first exclusively Jewish city in Palestine. Along with Jerusalem, it became a center of intense Zionist activity.

Between 1886 and 1914 the Arabs had launched attacks on most of the newly established settlements of the Yishuv—attacks that were repeated in 1920, 1921, 1929, 1936, and 1939. The new Arab nationalist movement was determined to stamp out any signs of a permanent Jewish settlement in Palestine.

The Jews slowly came to realize that they could not count on the British for their defense, so they made their agricultural settlements an integral part of their defense strategy. To this day each outpost, particularly those closest to Israel's borders, is sufficiently well armed to resist an invading Arab army until Jewish forces can arrive.

The choice of locations for these settlements was governed more by political and security considerations than economic or agricultural ones. For the leaders of the Haganah such settlements were designed not only to protect the Jewish state but also to define its borders.

By the spring of 1936 some 165 Jewish communities were spread across the country, from the heights of Galilee to the coastal plain and the valley of Jezreel. A decade later the number had grown to 270, complementing the equally large Jewish population growth in Jerusalem, Tel Aviv, and Haifa.

These farming settlements were divided into three categories, defined by their social and agricultural structure:

• The kibbutz, the international symbol of Israel's agricultural revolution; an Israeli invention and socioeconomic experiment that has worked only in Eretz Yisrael. Each kibbutz is a collective consisting of a single agricultural unit whose members have no private property and enjoy equal rights as well as equal obligations. The kibbutz meets the needs of its members by drawing from a collective economy. Children are lodged together, away from their parents.

• The moshav, a cooperative consisting of agricultural family units of equal size. Each farmer cultivates his own plot of land; hiring of paid labor is forbidden. The sale of produce and purchase of tools and equipment are made on a communal basis.

• The moshava, a village where the farmers own their own land and sell their produce independently.

The most idealistic young people joined kibbutzim, where life in a community of extremely modest conditions represented the true modern Jewish revolution. For them, khaki clothes and work blues were the height of luxury; in the kibbutz they could put into practice the egalitarian doctrines of Lenin and Trotsky without the political terror of Stalin.

The Zionist idealists who joined kibbutzim —and, to a large extent, moshavim—were often intellectuals in love with art and literature; they established the country's best schools, using avant-garde educational techniques. This combination of intelligence, culture, and hard work has given birth to some of the most remarkable figures in Israeli society and some of the army's greatest fighters.

Some of my favorite childhood memories are of the summer vacations I spent in Kibbutz Shaar Hagolan (the name means "Gate of the Golan") in the Jordan Valley. Its members, mostly Polish Jews, had built in the burning climate a thriving agricultural center based on carp and bananas. The kibbutz was an oasis of greenery and flowers; in the communal dining room we were served the milk and cream produced by the kibbutz cows.

The members, left-wing idealists, were firmly committed to peaceful coexistence with the Arabs. In its library one could find only leftist newspapers or such great Russian classics as *War and Peace, Anna Karenina,* and *The Brothers Karamazov,* all translated into Hebrew.

I was particularly jealous of the kibbutz children, who lived together in their own house. In the summer they would go barefoot on the black, burned earth. They knew the name of every plant, bird, and butterfly. They seemed more mature than my friends the same age back in the city. At a young age they learned how to ride horses.

But above all, it was the communal atmosphere—so different even from the tight-knit city communities—that I envied. After two months' vacation I would have to board the bus that would take me back to Tel Aviv. A wave of sadness would sweep over me as I saw the Sea of Galilee, the Jordan Valley, and Shaar Hagolan disappear until the following summer.

When in the 1930s the British as well as the

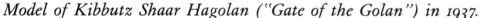

Model of Kibbutz Shaar Hagolan ("Gate of the Golan") in 1937.

*Construction of a kibbutz in the Negev,
1946–47.*

*Construction of a defense tower at Kibbutz
Shaar Hagolan.*

Arabs tried to halt the spread of Jewish settlements, the Haganah realized the need to devise new means of establishing new communities. Thus was born the method of watch-towers and enclosures.

Once engineers had approached the desig-

nated spot and built a road and irrigation canals, dozens of volunteers would prepare in secret, building in advance a barracks framework and wooden guard tower, along with the double-walled wooden enclosure which, when filled with earth and stones, was de-

December 1938: Sergeant Joseph Pressman of Kibbutz Ramat David disarms an Arab terrorist.

signed to shield the new settlement from Arab bullets. Before anything else, these defense posts would be hastily installed; when the Arabs, realizing the burst of new activity, attacked, the Jewish settlers were prepared.

Kibbutz Hanita, established on March 21, 1938, was the early symbol of this method's success. In just one day four hundred Haganah members, working on rough terrain recently purchased from the Arabs, installed a guard tower and enclosure that protected the new settlement from attack.

The operation, called "Eleven Points in the Negev," remains the highlight of the establishment of new settlements. In 1946, hearing that the Negev, then deserted save for a few Bedouin tribes, would be excluded from the Jewish state under the U.N. Partition Plan, the Jewish Agency and Haganah decided to act.

At the end of September, Golda Meir, head of the Jewish Agency's Political Department, drew up a Haganah plan to establish eleven new Negev settlements to join the seven kibbutzim already there. Such a plan was audacious, to say the least; under constant British surveillance, and with little means at their disposal, the Jews had to prepare in total secrecy.

Incredibly, the towers and enclosures of the eleven settlements were built in a single night —even before the installation of irrigation canals, so vital in the scorching desert region. In fact, facilities for water would not be put in for several months. The British first learned of the new settlements some thirty hours later when their agents saw the headlines in the Hebrew papers.

But these lonely outposts were to ensure Israel's possession of the Negev during the War of Independence.

Agricultural settlements also enabled the Yishuv to compensate for the disadvantage of its inferiority in numbers by providing simultaneous centers of settlement and defense, since the British had forbidden the Jews to establish an official armed force during the Mandate.

From the beginning of the Yishuv in the late nineteenth century until the establishment of the state, Jews were a minority in Palestine. In 1919 they numbered but 57,000 out of 590,000 inhabitants, less than 10 percent. A decade later, their numbers had nearly tripled—to 156,000—but they still constituted only 16 percent of the population. By the time immigration was halted by the British in 1939, there were 445,400 Jews in Eretz Yisrael;

A woman fighter of the Haganah in April 1948.

though their numbers had grown, the Arabs still outnumbered them by three to one.

Despite their minority status, the Jews never doubted their right to the land of Israel. As Ben-Gurion said in 1931, "The right to reconstruct with our hands the ruins of Eretz Yisrael depends neither on the acceptance nor on the refusal of the Arabs, and we will rise up against any power trying to make our rights dependent on the favor of the people living today in that land."

Despite Ben-Gurion's defense, it was obvious that the Jews would never enjoy political backing for control of the land until they possessed a majority of its inhabitants. The British knew that, too, which is why they at first limited and then stopped Jewish immigration.

But as the Yishuv slowly grew, its security was constantly threatened by the Arabs of Palestine. The ancient Jewish community in the holy city of Hebron, home of the Tomb of the Biblical Patriarchs, was all but annihilated by an Arab pogrom in 1929.

The Jews also felt the threat of the Arab population in the surrounding countries. On the eve of the War of Independence, Egypt had 22 million inhabitants, Syria 4 million, Transjordan 1 million, Lebanon 1.5 million, and Iraq and Saudi Arabia 6 million each.

Surrounded by these hostile nations, the territory allotted the Yishuv seemed even smaller by comparison and totally lacking in strategic depth. Its borders measured 654 miles in total length, and the topography of Judea and Samaria gave the Arab Legion a critical advantage in the battle for Jerusalem. At its narrowest point, less than 10 miles separated the Arab border town of Qalqilya from the Mediterranean coast.

The layout of the Yishuv was a strategic nightmare; the infant state could be easily cut into separate sections by a swift military operation. From their positions in the Golan Heights, the Syrians kept the Jewish communities in Galilee pinned down by fire.

In the years immediately preceding statehood, the Yishuv leaders carefully planned a system of agricultural settlements with an eye to these problems. The kibbutzim located in the extreme north of Galilee—Dan, Misgav Am, and Manara—protected every bit of land the Jews had been granted in the Partition Plan.

The Jewish Leadership

F ROM 1945 to 1948 three men were to distinguish themselves in the Jewish struggle against the British in Palestine: David Ben-Gurion, the acknowledged leader operating in the open, and the two controversial underground commanders Menachem Begin and Yitzhak Shamir. Each of the three would eventually become Prime Minister of the state he had helped found.

Of course, there were other key figures in Israel's birth struggle, particularly Golda Meir (then still named Myerson), who played a critical role in raising the desperately needed funds for Israel's first weapons purchases and who, as Israel's first ambassador to Moscow in 1948, instilled the first Zionist spirit in Soviet Jewry.

But from the start those three men were engaged in a fierce political rivalry and hostility whose repercussions are still felt in the young Jewish state today: Ben-Gurion and his

Golda Meir, David Ben-Gurion's right arm, in 1948.

David Ben-Gurion (1886–1973), "father" of the State of Israel.

followers on one side, Begin and Shamir and their partisans on the other.

In 1948 the leaders of the Jewish Agency considered Begin and Shamir outlaws, and their feelings barely changed once the state was firmly established. For decades Ben-Gurion even refused to acknowledge Begin's presence in the Knesset, the Israeli Parliament, repeatedly referring to him in debate as "the man sitting next to Knesset member Bader."

Not until 1967, on the eve of the Six-Day War, was Begin invited into a national-emergency coalition government by Levi Eshkol, Ben-Gurion's successor as Prime Minister. It took another seventeen years after that before Ben-Gurion's cherished disciple, Shimon Peres, agreed to share power with Shamir in a national unity government following deadlocked elections.

The differences between the two factions were philosophical and tactical; neither side questioned the other's commitment to Zionism and both sought the expulsion of the British from Palestine. But there was a fundamental difference over how this could—and should—be accomplished.

Ben-Gurion, known fondly by his followers as "the Old Man," led the moderate wing of revolutionary Zionism, which, essentially socialist in nature, was supported by most of the Yishuv. This faction stressed political negotiations and compromises over a direct armed struggle.

Ben-Gurion and his colleagues believed in the lightning-fast establishment of kibbutzim and moshavim to settle the country and arranged for the mass immigration of refugees, who they correctly realized would help render world opinion sympathetic to the Jewish cause.

A political leader who operated openly, Ben-Gurion was constantly in touch with the British High Commissioner in Palestine, even as his Haganah was grappling with British forces. In December 1946, given the Jewish Agency's defense portfolio, he attempted to reach a peaceful coexistence settlement with Palestine's Arab communities long before the British Mandate expired.

In sharp contrast, Begin and Shamir operated secretly; rather than being in touch with the authorities, they were hotly pursued by them. At various times, both men were fugitives with a British price on their heads. Their supporters attacked British camps and installa-

Menachem Begin in Poland.

tions and never hesitated to kill soldiers and police so that no Briton in Palestine could feel secure. For political reasons, Begin sometimes agreed to suspend operations against the British; for Shamir, it was a constant fight to the death.

As a child, I read the political broadsides posted on the walls of Tel Aviv by the Irgun and Lehi. Every operation was followed by a poster explaining the attack and the motivation behind it. Each poster invariably ended with the words "We will lay down our arms only after the last British soldier has left Palestine."

To suppress this rebellion, London dispatched 120,000 soldiers to the Holy Land—about one soldier for every five Jews. In Jerusalem the headquarters of the British Government—nicknamed "Bevingrad" for the anti-Zionist British Foreign Minister, Ernest Bevin—was fortified with barbed wire and tank traps. "Wanted" posters throughout the coun-

Twenty years later, Ben-Gurion and Begin are reconciled in the presence of Ezer Weizman.

try offered a generous reward for the capture of Begin and Shamir.

Begin directed the resistance from a modest apartment in Tel Aviv. He grew a thick beard and wore the trappings of an Orthodox Jew, assuming the identity of one Rabbi Israel Sassover. Shamir tried the same disguise, but less successfully—his thick eyebrows betrayed him. He was deported to a British prison camp in Africa, along with hundreds of other Irgun and Sternist fighters. But Shamir managed to escape; traveling by way of present-day Somalia and Djibouti, he arrived on board a French ship in Toulon just two weeks before the establishment of the state.

I was to come to know both men well, particularly in recent years. Whenever I was in the company of Menachem Begin or Yitzhak Shamir, I felt I was in the presence of an exceptional being with extraordinary tenacity. Like Ben-Gurion, both men were consumed by the idea that it was in their hands to prevent a second Holocaust.

Few accused terrorists have become heads of state following a revolution—especially in those days—and it is safe to say that never in

Begin becomes leader of the Irgun in 1943.

their worst nightmares did Ben-Gurion and Golda Meir dream that Begin and Shamir would approach the reins of power in Israel, let alone follow in their footsteps as Prime Minister.

Both were convinced that each outrage committed by the underground against the British prevented an efficient campaign to win Jewish independence. Ben-Gurion charged that the Irgun and Lehi needlessly exacerbated tensions with London, which led to an unwelcome police crackdown in Palestine.

Each of these dynamic leaders was absolutely convinced that he alone possessed the magic formula that would drive the British from Palestine and reestablish the Jewish state.

Ben-Gurion, Begin, and Shamir had at least two things in common: All three were born in Poland—Ben-Gurion in 1886, Begin in 1913, and Shamir in 1915. And all three came to Eretz Yisrael convinced that a Jewish state would take root there.

But from there, the differences took over. Begin and Shamir, like the rest of Jabotinsky's Revisionists, believed the Jewish state would include all of the original territory of Palestine on both sides of the Jordan River. Ben-Gurion, more pragmatic, was prepared to compromise, limiting the state's borders in return for its mere existence.

The stocky Ben-Gurion, whose wild mane of white hair became his trademark and who never felt comfortable in a jacket and tie, was both stubborn and energetic—and he refused to be contradicted by anyone.

The slim Begin, always elegant and attired in a suit, looked the part he had been trained to play, that of a gentleman Polish lawyer and scholar. Unlike Ben-Gurion, however, he tended toward heavy emotion, sometimes even hysteria. Paradoxically, his public nature was in sharp contrast to the silent, secret methods of his organization; he believed in speeches as much as in operations. But then, Begin was never a tactical organizer; his function was to spread the Irgun's political message.

Ben-Gurion also liked to make speeches, but he preferred deeds: another new settlement, another boatload of immigrants. Shamir and his group complemented each other; he was by far the quietest of the three, rarely making speeches, and even today his speaking style lacks the fiery tirades of Begin.

But in sharp contrast to his two rivals, Shamir was more than a leader—he was a joiner. Never content with sitting safely on the sidelines, this robust little man took part directly in many Stern Group operations.

Ben-Gurion withdrew from the political arena in 1963 at age seventy-seven, retiring to the tranquillity of Kibbutz Sde Boker in the Negev. Begin, haunted by the controversy over the war in Lebanon and the tragic death of his devoted wife, abruptly quit as Prime Minister and remained secluded in his Jerusalem apartment in 1983, at age seventy.

The seventy-two-year-old Shamir, who first entered politics at the age of fifty-five after a career in intelligence, is at this writing the Prime Minister and is expected to preside over Israel's fortieth birthday celebration.

Running the Blockade

BLOCKADE RUNNING became one of the Jews' most important and effective weapons. The British, under Arab pressure, tried to stop the blockade runners from the beginning, for it was clear to the Arabs that if the Jews succeeded in increasing their numbers in Palestine, their claim to the land would be strengthened.

The voyage of the *Exodus* in 1947 was the climax of Jewish struggle to reach the Promised Land by circumventing British regulations and policies. Virtually from the start, the British restricted the number of Jews permitted to enter Palestine. The Jews, however, tried to reach the country by every means possible. In the early years they came as tourists who never left, or they slipped across the Lebanese border to the north. It was an unorganized form of immigration by individuals and groups.

With Hitler's rise to power in 1933, the situation took a dramatic turn. Jews from Germany and central Europe sought a place of refuge. When they decided to abandon their homes and businesses—and the European cit-ies in which they had lived for generations— Palestine seemed to many to be the safest place as Hitler's threatening shadow continued to lengthen.

The British, however, imposed strict limitations on Jewish entry into Palestine through small, fixed quotas. So the Jews started looking for organized ways of bringing their brethren to Palestine. Beginning in 1934, they purchased ships and boats on which hundreds of Jews could be transported. Members of the Haganah would meet the boats at a remote

Illegal immigrants during the 1930s.

beach, before a British patrol happened by, and slip the refugees ashore. This Irgun Aliyah Bet (Immigration B Organization), or Mosad Aliyah Bet, slowly grew as the Haganah's clandestine organization for bringing Jewish immigrants to Palestine.

Zev Jabotinsky, perhaps the most outstanding and certainly the most controversial of the Zionist leaders, explained the issue clearly in his May 1939 article "The National Sport": "The National Sport, which I heartily recommend to Jewish youth, is called 'free immigration.' The Jewish National Sport helps millions of hungry souls break through a gate which is otherwise closed to them. It helps in acquiring a homeland for a homeless mass and in transforming them into a nation. Other types of sports are ultimately nothing but games. Our sport has a sacred seriousness."

Between 1934 and the outbreak of World War II in 1939, various Jewish organizations brought dozens of ships to the country. In several cases the ship would approach the beaches of Tel Aviv only to be stranded on a reef or sandbank. Haganah men would rush to unload the passengers and disperse them among the residents of Tel Aviv, the first exclusively Jewish city in Eretz Yisrael. It is estimated that up to 35,000 Jews slipped into Eretz Yisrael aboard illegal immigration ships.

British naval patrols were not yet prepared to cope with this new phenomenon. It would be eight more years before the British became capable of organizing the enormous naval force needed to block the trail of the *Exodus* and its sister ships. The British Coast Guard prevented only a small number of ships from reaching the shores of Palestine; they could not hold back the human tide along the beaches.

That such a relatively large number of Jews arrived in Palestine illegally during the 1930s indicates how clearly the Jews of Europe— Poland and Germany in particular—sensed

48

November 16, 1947: The English deport Haifa's illegal immigrants to Cyprus.

the ground burning under their feet. Many more could have been saved had the British allowed Jews to enter Palestine freely. Very possibly hundreds of thousands and perhaps millions of Jews would have been saved before they fell into the vicious hands of the Nazis.

The British, however, did not ease up on their opposition to Jewish immigration because of the growing Nazi horror stories. In fact, they became even more stringent. In May 1939, four months before the outbreak of war, the British caved in to Arab pressure and published the infamous White Paper imposing severe restrictions on the Jews' ability to purchase land or settle in Palestine. Above all, the White Paper stated that all Jewish immigration to Palestine would cease within five years, "unless the Arabs of Palestine are prepared to acquiesce in it."

These restrictions shocked the Jews, both in Eretz Yisrael and abroad. They considered these measures a betrayal of the 1917 Balfour Declaration committing the British to establish a Jewish homeland in Palestine, and a signal of British intent to give the country to the Arabs. Above all else, there was a feeling that the British had condemned European Jews to extermination.

October 30, 1947: Deportation of illegal immigrants to Cyprus.

March 26, 1945: Illegal immigrants following their deportation by the British to the island of Mauritius.

Across Palestine, thousands demonstrated against the Mandatory government. Behind the scenes, however, the Jews took practical steps. Shaul Avigur, one of the outstanding commanders of the Haganah, was appointed head of the illegal immigration organization. Avigur proved himself to be a master of clandestine operations and an excellent organizer. He was a Zionist revolutionary firmly resolved to do everything possible to break the British blockade. His memories of the pogroms against Jews in Russia, where he had been born in 899, served as an added impetus.

twentieth century. It was his fleet of ships that brought Jewish refugees to Eretz Yisrael.

The Second World War, which began with the German forces marching into Poland on September 1, 1939, triggered the flight of thousands of Jewish refugees across Europe. Only a small number ever made it to the underground ships waiting to ferry them to Eretz Yisrael. From Poland, Germany, Romania, and Bulgaria, countless numbers desperately sought ways of reaching Eretz Yisrael.

Even the war did not change Britain's resolve to bar Jewish entry into Palestine. Many of those who succeeded in making their way to the shores of Eretz Yisrael found themselves sent to British detainment camps or deported to the island of Mauritius in the Indian Ocean. The Haganah tried, usually in vain, to prevent the deportations. On November 25, 1940, when the British had placed 1,800 refugees on the deportation ship *Patria* in the port of Haifa, the Haganah smuggled explosives on board to blow up the ship's engines. But the operation ended in disaster: The *Patria* sank, and about 260 people drowned below

Avigur was twelve when he immigrated to Palestine with his family. From the beginning he was involved in settling the land and defending Jewish settlements that came under Arab attack. "I believe in actions no matter how insignificant they may be and not in highfalutin talk and speeches," Avigur repeatedly stated. He was one of the founders of the Kinneret group, a Jewish agricultural commune—but he was born to be a member of a clandestine organization. Avigur established, with meager resources and in total secrecy, the largest shadow fleet in the history of the

Jaffa, October 27, 1933: British policemen (background) during an Arab demonstration against Jewish immigration.

Mount Carmel, opposite the very shores on which the refugees had not been allowed to set foot.

The mass drowning of helpless refugees caused British public opinion to recoil in shock even as the Jews' hatred reached new heights. The authorities in London finally relented, agreeing to let the *Patria*'s survivors remain in Palestine in a detention camp at Atlit.

The *Patria* was a tragic but dramatic dress rehearsal for what would happen in the same place seven years later on board the *Exodus*.

The war, which by now had spread to the Mediterranean, endangered the passage of the rickety ships carrying Jewish refugees. Many were trying to flee Romania, in which a pro-Nazi regime had been established. In 1942 Romanian Jewish refugees set sail for Eretz Yisrael aboard the *Struma*. On February 23 the ship sank; only one of the 769 on board survived.

Remarkably, the disasters at sea did not de-

ter the clandestine ships. To the Jews of Eretz Yisrael, saving even one of their brethren was an achievement. All told, Aliyah Bet brought 20,000 refugees to Eretz Yisrael during the war, aboard thirteen ships. Admittedly, this figure is pitiful compared to that of the 6 million Jews who were exterminated. It should not, however, be forgotten that they were saved at a time when most of Europe was being crushed beneath the Nazi jackboot. Moreover, the Jews in Eretz Yisrael had very limited resources with which to save their brethren, and they also had to operate underground to defy the British authorities.

When the magnitude of the Holocaust became known, Palestine Jewry's rage toward the British knew no bounds. As more and more details about the extermination of millions of Jews in the gas chambers and ovens of Auschwitz, Treblinka, and Majdanek were revealed, the fury toward those who had closed the gates of freedom and safety intensified even more.

Face to Face
with the Holocaust

THE VICTORY over Hitler brought the Jews of Palestine face to face with the knowledge of the most highly planned and sophisticated death machine mankind has ever known. The human skeletons discovered in Auschwitz, the crematoria in which millions of people were burned at Treblinka, Majdanek, and other camps, all told the horrifying story of the extermination of one third of the Jewish people. Entire Jewish communities, from Warsaw to Berlin, were eradicated. Hundreds of thousands of Jews from Budapest to Paris, from Salonika to Lvov, were liquidated by the Germans.

The documents and oral testimony presented at Nuremberg, where the first Nazi war criminals were tried, showed how the Germans had coldly plotted the extermination of the Jews. It was there that Adolf Eichmann was publicly named for the first time as the man to whom Hitler and his henchmen had assigned overall responsibility for the organized genocide.

The court found that the mass murder had been carried out by a variety of means: "shooting, hanging, suffocation by gas, starvation, systematic malnutrition, kicking, beating, acts of cruelty and torture of all kinds, the pulling out of fingernails and the conduct of experiments on living persons. . . ." The German criminals, the court found, "knowingly and systematically committed genocide, the destruction of ethnic groups and races, primarily Jews and Poles, as well as gypsies and others."

The evidence at Nuremberg confirmed that the leaders of the Third Reich had prepared a detailed "Final Solution" of the Jewish "problem." "Beginning in June 1943," the court found, "the Germans took steps to hide the evidence of their crimes. They withdrew bodies from graves, and burned them and ground up their bones by machine to turn them into agricultural fertilizer. . . ."

IVB4, a special office in the Reichssicherheitshauptamt (Main Office for Reich Security), was responsible for the extermination of the Jews. Obersturmbannführer Adolf Eichmann was in charge of this office.

In Auschwitz alone, as many as two and a

54

half million people were exterminated, and a half million others died of hunger and illness between May 1940 and December 1, 1943. In a sworn affidavit signed on April 5, 1946, Rudolf Hoess, commandant of Auschwitz, testified: ". . . All told three million people died . . . the victims included about 100,000 German Jews and large numbers of other nationals, mostly Jews, from Holland, France, Belgium, Poland, Hungary, Greece, and other countries. In the summer of 1944 alone, we put 400,000 Hungarian Jews to death at Auschwitz. . . . The mass murder by gas began in 1941 and continued until the fall of 1944. . . . I myself was in command of the killings in Auschwitz until December 1, 1943, and subsequently continued in a supervisory role in the concentration camps. . . . The 'Final Solution' of the Jewish question meant the complete destruction of all the Jews of Europe. . . . The commander of the Treblinka camp told me that he had exterminated 80,000 people in six months. He was involved primarily in the liquidation of the Jews from the Warsaw Ghetto. He used monoxide gas and in my opinion his methods were not very effective. Therefore, when I started the extermination in Auschwitz, I used a crystal flake acid, Zyklon B [prussic acid]. . . . We knew when people had died, because their screaming stopped. . . ."

In the testimony on the number of Jews murdered, SS Captain Dieter Wisliceny, one of Eichmann's aides, told the court in Nuremberg on January 3, 1946, that "Eichmann himself always spoke of at least four million Jews. At times he spoke of five million. . . . He said that he would leap into his grave laughing, because he would particularly enjoy the feeling that five million people were on his

Survivors of Nazi concentration camps in Austria (Ebensee).

Concentration camp internees symbolically break the barbed wire of their camps.

conscience. . . ." Eichmann's cynical statement gave further impetus to the Mosad agents who set out to kidnap him years later.

The Jews of Eretz Yisrael did not have to wait for the Nuremberg trials to learn of the most horrifying event in their people's long history. Palestinian Jewish soldiers serving in the British Army saw survivors with their own eyes and brought their stories home with them. The word "catastrophe" did not begin to describe the tragedy. The Hebrew word "Shoah" ("Holocaust") entered the tortured vocabulary of the Jews. Even those who speak Hebrew well have difficulty at times comprehending the full significance of the meaning.

I remember myself as a child of ten standing in the kitchen of my home in Tel Aviv holding my mother's apron and trying to comfort her as she broke down in bitter tears. In her hand was a letter.

"Why are you crying?" I asked.

"The Germans murdered them, all of them," she sobbed. "They sent my whole family to Auschwitz. They killed all the Jews in Poland."

The letter was from my aunt, my mother's sister, the only surviving member of an entire family that had been sent to Auschwitz. I remember the picture in the envelope. It showed a young woman dressed in the striped uniform of a concentration camp.

My father, a native of Salonika in Greece, told me the same terrible story. His entire family had been wiped out at Auschwitz.

Immigrants to Palestine display their tattoos from the Nazi camps

They were among the nearly 50,000 residents of that city sent there by Adolf Eichmann.

My mother and father had arrived in Palestine in the 1930s, a few years before the outbreak of the Second World War. They were Zionists, who believed in Theodor Herzl's philosophy, and for that reason they remained alive.

As a child I could not fully comprehend the magnitude of the catastrophe. I am barely able to today. But for the Jewish leaders in Eretz Yisrael this was the final straw. The Holocaust became the detonator for the Zionist explosive. After the first shock came the fury: fury at the Germans, and fury at the British.

The fury against the Germans took the form of Haganah squads who hunted Nazis across Europe and killed them without trial. In those days the hunt for Adolf Eichmann and other Nazis had already begun.

The bitter resentment toward the British stemmed from the 1939 White Paper that closed the gates to Eretz Yisrael during the years in which so much of European Jewry could have been saved. The heads of the Haganah, and the Irgun and Stern Group as well —indeed, the whole Jewish population of Eretz Yisrael—blamed the British for having blocked the rescue of Jews from their horrible enemy.

Saving the Shearith Hapletah, as the survivors of the concentration camps came to be known, became the supreme objective of the Jews of Eretz Yisrael. The way to do this was to bring them home. The Haganah sent Aliyah Bet agents to Europe to organize clandestine transportation to Eretz Yisrael. They were assisted by Haganah members serving in the British Army who had not yet been demo-

The arrival in Haifa of Buchenwald survivors on July 15, 1945. They were later arrested by the British.

Immigrants to Palestine wearing the yellow Star of David.

bilized. Together they smuggled groups of refugees over European borders and placed them aboard ships bound for Eretz Yisrael.

The whole world was shocked and stunned by the death camps, but the government of Great Britain decided that the gates of Eretz Yisrael would remain closed, with only very small quotas of Jews granted entry. The Arabs of the Middle East were far too important to the empire's interests.

Ironically, it was this callousness that eventually hastened the end of Britain's rule in Palestine. What had happened to Pharaoh three thousand years earlier now happened to the British Government. Just as Pharaoh refused to allow the Hebrews to leave Egypt for the land of Israel until God punished him with ten plagues, so the Jews punished the British Empire with the "plague" of illegal immigration and burst through the closed gates to Eretz Yisrael.

The King David Hotel

T HE HOSTILITY between the Haganah on the one hand and the Irgun and Lehi on the other was so strong that the fighters of Begin and Shamir were convinced they had more to fear from David Ben-Gurion than from the British. Ben-Gurion had been very explicit: "It is either us or them; Zionism, the Yishuv, the Jewish people or the Irgun and Lehi. There cannot be any neutrality."

An atmosphere of fratricidal war swept the country. Begin, disguised as a young rabbi, fled from village to village with his wife, Aliza, and young son to hide from the combined vigilance of their Jewish brothers and the British, who had offered a ten-thousand-pound reward for him—"dead or alive."

Ben-Gurion's camp hoped that Winston Churchill's government in London would, in a gesture of postwar generosity and compassion over the horrors of the Holocaust, grant

The King David Hotel after the explosion on July 22, 1946; the dead and wounded are removed from the debris.

A search being carried out in a kibbutz by British troops for weapons belonging to the Haganah.

the Jews statehood, even if only in part of historical Palestine. This wishful thinking was strengthened when Clement Attlee's Labour Party stunned Churchill's Conservatives in Britain's first postwar election. Ben-Gurion and his colleagues, outspoken Socialists, were convinced that the members of the new leftist government, who had always been supportive of Zionism, would act in the name of socialist solidarity.

So convinced was the Jewish Agency of the inevitability of statehood that, rather than jeopardize relations with London, its leaders ordered the Haganah to stop all anti-British actions by the Irgun and Stern Group; indeed, Ben-Gurion sent special Haganah units out to kidnap Jewish "terrorists." Many Irgunists and Sternists were tortured by their Jewish brothers to divulge the location of arms caches; once they talked, the Haganah delivered them into British hands.

Thus, even before statehood, the Jews were divided among themselves. Begin, though furious over the Haganah actions, refused to sanction retaliation; he did not want to send Jew against Jew, even as the Haganah weak-

ened his organization and diminished effectiveness against the common foe, the British.

But once he became Prime Minister, the pro-Zionist Attlee forgot his past promises. He handed over the Foreign Ministry to the fiercely anti-Zionist Ernest Bevin, who immediately pushed for stronger ties with Arab communities and cracked down on Jewish immigration to the Holy Land.

This was the detonator. In a rare show of cooperation and unity, the Haganah, Irgun, and Lehi decided to join together in a mutual action against the British, although the Haganah reserved the right to veto any operation.

Thus, for a pitifully short time, came into being the Jewish Revolt movement.*

It was the highlight of the Jewish struggle against the British. In one night the railroads of Palestine were sabotaged at 180 separate points. On another night, in February 1946, all three major British Air Force bases were attacked. At one installation the young Irgun combatants destroyed twenty-eight heavy bombers. In another operation, this one carried out by the Haganah, all the bridges connecting Palestine to its neighbors were destroyed; this became known as "the Night of the Bridges," and fourteen Haganah fighters lost their lives.

Despite these losses, the movement continued and grew strong. Irgun combatants disguised as British soldiers penetrated British bases, often in broad daylight, and carried off cases of arms and ammunition. In desperation, the British dispatched reinforcements—and decreed that any Jew found carrying arms would risk the death penalty.

But the struggle had gained its first objective: awakening world opinion. In the United

* British general elections took place in July 1945, bringing the Labour Party to power. On October 25, 1945, agreement was reached by all clandestine Jewish organizations in Palestine to set up a Jewish Revolt movement and to go on the offensive. Operations started in November the same year. The Haganah not only in practice but also formally withdrew from this arrangement at the end of August 1946.

An arrest is made during the curfew.

States and Britain, large headlines and long articles covered the exploits of the Palestinian Jewish underground. And while London's newspaper editorials were uniformly hostile, they began to carry a message to the government: "Get out of Palestine."

Under this pressure the Attlee regime sent an Anglo-American Commission of Inquiry to Palestine. At the same time, on June 29, 1946, the Mandatory authorities launched a new offensive against the Yishuv. On that Saturday, since known in Zionist annals as "Black Sabbath," British soldiers and police surrounded dozens of kibbutzim and moshavim known to be Haganah strongholds. There they arrested three thousand young men,

mostly Palmach members, and sent them to a special detention camp near Latrun. They also arrested the entire leadership of the Jewish Agency, save Ben-Gurion, who was then in Paris.

With their trained dogs, the British discovered many arms caches, particularly at Kibbutz Yagur, which held the Haganah's main arsenal in the north.

The Yishuv was in a state of paralysis. Opponents of armed struggle felt justified in their belief that military actions would never open the gates of Palestine; indeed, they had prompted an unprecedented British attack that had all but neutralized the Haganah.

For this reason the Haganah decided to end

63

its cooperation with the Irgun and Lehi, focusing instead on clandestine immigration and the acquisition of arms. On July 22, 1946, in an action that rocked the world, that cooperation ended forever.

In coordination with the still-existing Revolt movement, Menachem Begin had decided to bomb the King David Hotel in Jerusalem and destroy the wing used by the British as headquarters for the First Secretary of the Mandatory government. Other offices in the same wing of the Middle East's most luxurious hotel housed British Army and Air Force intelligence and the prosecutors who had brought about the death sentence for so many Jewish fighters. In the basement the British had installed their military communications center.

Irgun agents, dressed in the white jellebas of the hotel's Sudanese waiters, penetrated the King David's kitchen carrying large milk jars stuffed with explosives. As they were leaving, there was some exchange of gunfire when it was realized that the waiters were phony. But the British never considered a possible bomb plot.

The Irgun had decided to issue a warning before the explosion so that the hotel could be evacuated in time. In the half hour before the explosion the Irgun made three different calls warning that the hotel should be evacuated. But there had been other bomb threats—and the British authorities refused to heed the warning.

The resulting explosion could be heard for miles around. The entire British wing of the hotel was destroyed, and with it some ninety people, including Arabs and Jews as well as high British officials. It was the death of these civilians that led the Haganah to condemn the operation publicly and label Menachem Begin a "terrorist"—a stigma he would carry for decades.

But the attack on the King David remains unequaled among resistance operations. The repercussions were felt in Jerusalem, in London, and around the world as attention was focused on the problems of Palestine.

Begin, however, remained agonized by the civilian deaths; up until then the Irgun had struck almost exclusively at military targets. This time civilians became the victims. He would send one note of condolence and apology: to the Palestinian correspondent of the New York *Post,* then the only pro-Irgun newspaper in the United States.

Animosity between the Haganah and Irgun also deepened. The British hurried two divisions to Tel Aviv, encircled its two thousand inhabitants, and declared a general curfew as they began a house-to-house search for Irgun members.

I still remember the British soldiers entering our home without knocking. The mustached commanding officer pointed his revolver at my father while we were eating supper. I was deeply disturbed that the officer, apparently drunk, was waving his gun a mere three feet from my father's face. Only after verifying his identity card would the soldiers leave.

It was during that curfew operation that the British found and arrested Yitzhak Shamir. Despite the disguise of his rabbinical beard, he was betrayed by the bushy eyebrows that even now are his physical trademark.

From the time of the King David affair, the British increased their use of a new weapon against the Irgun and the Stern Group: the gallows.

Shaul Avigur
Yossi Harel

HOVERING like an enormous shadow over the most secret of the Haganah's actions is the legend of Shaul Avigur. As much as Ben-Gurion, he stimulated and inspired the political leaders of the Yishuv. It was Avigur who persuaded them that not only must illegal immigration and arms purchases abroad continue, but the Jews could produce their own weapons in secret workshops.

Throughout his life he jealously guarded his privacy and anonymity, constantly fending off personal publicity even after statehood. As a result, sadly, few Israelis know today of the critical role he played as the number two man in the defense first of the Yishuv and then of the young state.

Shaul Avigur was a modest man who lived an ascetic life. Among his Haganah colleagues he had a reputation for incredible courage; he was able to make the most difficult decisions calmly and rationally. Most important, he had a knack for clandestine activities; it was said jokingly that he refused to tell taxi drivers his destination because it was a state secret.

Avigur waged a war of wits with British intelligence on two fronts: organizing illegal immigration ships, and arranging for secret shipments of arms from Europe. Illegal immigration, he said, was "the train that we Jews are pushing on the rails of history."

His most famous operation was the *Exodus,* and the man he chose to command it, one who had already distinguished himself in other missions, was Yossi Hamburger, a fifth-generation Jerusalemite, who was to change his last name to Harel. Under Avigur, Harel commanded four ships which, following World War II, brought twenty-five thousand Jewish refugees to Eretz Yisrael.

Young Yossi Hamburger was only nine years old at the time of a bloody Arab pogrom that devastated the tiny Jewish community of Motza, near Jerusalem. Swearing that he would do whatever he could to prevent such a tragedy from happening again, he joined the Haganah at age fourteen, where his col-

Shaul Avigur, founder of Mosad Aliyah Bet.

leagues included Moshe Dayan and Yigal Allon. Within a few short years, he would be the Haganah's youngest officer.

One of his first missions was at Kibbutz Hanita, a critical outpost that would later help determine Israel's frontier. Yossi was sent as a Haganah instructor to help organize the new village's defense against armed Arab attacks.

Later, he was among the Haganah men who met illegal immigration ships on the beaches, rushing the refugees into the different villages and towns before they could be captured by the British. That activity led him to join the naval forces of the Palmach. The main course there was swimming. Yossi trained himself by swimming in the Jordan River, thus preparing himself for the struggle on the high seas. Later the young fighters were trained in navigation and canoeing.

When World War II broke out, Harel was one of many Haganah soldiers who volunteered to help fight the Nazis; he joined the British Royal Air Force as a gunner and spent two years battling the Germans, first in Greece and later at Lake Habbaniya, Iraq.

Returning to Palestine in 1941, he was made a weapons instructor in the Palmach and soon became a sabotage specialist for Haganah teams operating behind enemy lines. In 1943 he was appointed liaison officer between the Haganah and Dr. Chaim Weizmann, Herzl's successor as leader of the world Zionist movement. Weizmann, himself a world-renowned scientist, often told Harel, "You will be fortunate enough to see the Jewish state; I won't. Without science, there will be no state." Weizmann was overpessimistic. He became Israel's first President, and the Weizmann Institute at Rehovot, which has become one of the most important research centers in the world, bears his name.

Weizmann told Harel how, having seen aerial photos of Nazi death camps, he pleaded with Prime Minister Winston Churchill to send British planes to bomb the crematoria and halt, even if only temporarily, the German factories for killing. Churchill's answer, Weizmann complained bitterly, was that Britain had only enough bombs for vital military objectives.

Between 1945 and 1948 the Haganah ferried 84,333 illegal immigrants in some seventy ships in an attempt to run the British blockade.

After the war, Harel was sent to Greece with a suitcase containing a quarter of a million dollars. His orders: to buy a ship. With the gold in his possession, Harel and his comrades bought two cargo ships that had been refloated in the port of Piraeus after having been sunk.

One of these ships, renamed the *Knesset Yisrael* by its new commander, reached Yugoslavia, where authorities allowed him to pick

At left in this photo of peaceful vacationers: Yossi Harel.

up three thousand Jewish refugees. From the tortured mouths of his Hungarian and Romanian passengers, Harel heard first-hand of the Nazi horrors. His hatred for the British flaring, Harel vowed to smash their blockade of Palestine.

"We had the feeling that saving these refugees was our most sacred mission," he recalled much later. "Crowded aboard the ship, they cried and sang the Zionist anthem 'Hatikvah' . . . yes, they cried and they sang."

The *Knesset Yisrael* took on an additional nine hundred refugees from another boat that had sunk in the Adriatic off the Yugoslavian coast. In the port of Split, bakers worked for a day and a half to cook enough bread to avert starvation on board.

The 1,800-ton vessel, with coal-powered engines and a pitiful maximum speed of five knots, headed for Palestine. For the first time, Harel would confront the British on the high seas; the experience would serve him well later on board the *Exodus*.

In the cold November winds, the six-day journey would take the *Knesset Yisrael* twenty-three days. Despite rules forbidding women more than eight months' pregnant from boarding the ship, there were eight

Jewish immigrants being deported by the British to Cyprus.

births during the trip. One took place off the Peloponnesian Peninsula, but the infant died after twelve hours. Years later, recalling the tragedy as if it were fresh in his mind, Harel would describe the funeral at sea: how he attached a chain to weight down the infant's body, which had been placed in a makeshift wooden coffin.

"It was terrible," he said. "Is there anything purer than a baby that has just been born? Even to this day, every time I touch a rusty chain I remember that child. I can still taste on my lips the spray of the salty wave that carried that infant into the depths. It was the first death I witnessed on board a refugee ship."

On the *Exodus,* the cost in lives would be much higher.

A violent storm threatened to shipwreck the *Knesset Yisrael* on the coast, but luckily it abated. The regular crew slipped off the ship to avoid arrest by the British, leaving an undermanned Jewish crew; toward the end the refugees themselves shoveled the coal to power the ship.

As the ship passed the Turkish coast on its course for Palestine, a British bomber appeared. Before long the *Knesset Yisrael* was surrounded by four destroyers. The fuel ran out off the coast of Lebanon; the passengers ripped apart wooden bunks to feed the boilers.

November 26, 1946: illegal immigrants are deported to British camps in Cyprus.

68

Yossi Harel walking at Chaim Weizmann's right shoulder (Weizmann center, in hat).

But when the British forced the ship into the port of Haifa and attempted to board her, they were confronted by twelve hundred refugees wielding truncheons. For forty minutes the two forces were locked in a stalemate. Then the British fired tear gas.

"It was hell," recalled Harel. "Gas grenades landed in the stern, where the women and children had been grouped together. Their screams were harrowing; many jumped overboard to escape the gas. Meanwhile the British attacked in waves, trying to force the refugees off the ship.

"My blood was boiling. This was a new type of war: not a battle with arms but a terrible, humiliating battle. The British treated us as if we were subhuman."

Yossi Harel was the last to leave the ship. Taken into custody, he was sent to a prison camp on Cyprus. For months he would relive the bitter battle in the port of Haifa.

After escaping from Cyprus, Harel made his way back to Palestine. At twenty-eight he was ready for his next mission. The orders were to come soon: commander of the *Exodus.*

Exodus

By Yossi Harel

The War at Sea

I T WAS FRIDAY, July 11, 1947. I still remember every instant of that balmy morning when my ship, the *Exodus,* ran aground just a few yards from the open sea that would take us to the shores of the Promised Land, to Palestine. To Eretz Yisrael. The first mate steering the ship had made a mistake. As we approached the breakwater at the exit of the French port of Sète, the ship should have turned left. Instead, it veered right. We felt a mighty jolt; moments later, we were stuck on a sandbank.

Those were the longest minutes of my life. Foremost in my thoughts were the 4,515 Jewish refugees occupying the *Exodus.* Children, women, the elderly, the sick, they had all miraculously survived the Nazi ovens—only to be stuck on this reef in the port of Sète.

Their utter exhaustion and helplessness was buoyed by one great hope: that this ship would carry them to the land of their own.

The crowd of immigrants gathers on the deck of the Exodus, *July 18, 1947.*

Front page of Le Provençal, *July 31, 1947, headlining (left) the three prison ships off Port-de-Bouc.*

They were the largest single contingent of Jews ever to travel to the land of Israel since the Exodus from Egypt two thousand years earlier.

We quickly began making calculations of how many boats would be needed to get all the refugees off the ship. Thoughts raced wildly through my mind; the friends we had left behind on the dock must have been shattered to see us stranded on the sandbank after all the efforts and difficulties we had been through. Perhaps they had already reported this reverse to Shaul Avigur, commander of Aliyah Bet, who was in Paris awaiting news.

As for the British secret service, whose agents were swarming all over the port and whose destroyers were waiting for us out at sea, they were no doubt delighted that the refugee ship, whose movements they had followed with eager interest for many months, was now helplessly stuck.

Our feelings at that moment went beyond the *Exodus*—it was as if our whole massive effort of immigration had been stopped in its tracks. This was real war, our war at sea. More than 2,600 Jews had been drowned on the numerous voyages to Eretz Yisrael since 1935.

In crucial and difficult moments of decision such as these, one often has to take unorthodox steps. We decided to try to get the *Exodus* off the reef by exploiting her own power. She had excellent engines, and we opened them up to full throttle. The whole vessel shuddered and shook. Women and children cringed in fear on their wooden bunks. They felt something had gone wrong—that their fate hinged on what would happen in the next few minutes.

Inch by inch the engines of the *Exodus* plowed through the sandbar. We paid no attention to anything or anyone—not the French watching from the quay, nor the British destroyers lying in wait for us on the high seas. Suddenly, after an hour that seemed more like an eternity, we felt the boat floating again. What a marvelous feeling! We quickly checked the ship and found that its hull had miraculously come through unscathed.

I immediately sent a message, signed with my code name "Amnon," to a worried Shaul Avigur in Paris that the *Exodus* was under way. Later, I was told, he had sighed with relief that "the telegram arrived in the nick of time."

This is how the voyage of the refugee ship that became the symbol of the Jewish struggle for statehood began. "Exodus," which for generations has signified the deliverance of the Jews from Pharaoh's Egypt to the land of Canaan, had again become a magic word. "Exodus 1947" signified the deliverance of the remnant of European Jewry, saved from the hands of a modern pharaoh, the most vicious in history.

When I first set eyes on the *Exodus,* she was known as the *President Warfield.* I was in Italy as an emissary of the Haganah, the largest, most important, and most organized of the Jewish underground movements.

It was 1947, and I was engaged in weapons smuggling. One day that spring, I received a message that Shaul Avigur, the commander of Aliyah Bet, wanted to see me. He arrived in Italy from his office in Paris. We met immediately in a small coffee shop near the Piazza Duomo in Milan. He ordered coffee for me— but no cake. We spoke Hebrew so that no one could understand us. Shaul told me that a ship had arrived in Portofino and was being prepared to sail to Palestine. "Since you have

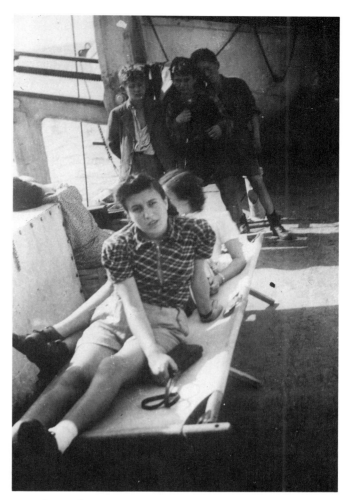

During the voyage to Haifa.

had experience with the ship *Knesset Yisrael,* you will be given command of this ship," he said. "She will carry 4,500 people. When can you be ready?" "Right now!" I replied.

Within an hour I was on the road to Portovenere, near La Spezia, accompanied by Avigur and Ada Sireni, the Haganah's brave representative in Italy, who knew everyone who was anyone in the Rome government. In Portovenere, I first saw the big ship with its massive smokestack. Her upper section was made of wood. The *President Warfield,* purchased with funds from the Jewish community of Baltimore, had originally been a pleasure vessel, plying the rivers of the United States.

Shaul introduced me as the ship's commander to the members of the crew, most of

Some of the 655 children who were aboard the Exodus.

whom were American Jews; the captain was Ike Aronovitch.

I wandered around the ship, carefully inspecting her. Originally, she'd had 120 cabins for 120 passengers, but an Italian crew was already busy taking apart the cabins and preparing wooden bunks that would accommodate 4,500 refugees lying down. A crew, headed by Avraham Zakai, made up of members of the Palmach—the elite strike force of the Haganah—supervised the complicated and involved refurbishments. It was necessary to prepare large kitchens, first aid stations, toilets, and showers, and to do so quickly and secretly.

But the British intervened. Not only did they hold the strings to our own land, they were quite influential in postwar Italy. The British ordered the Italians to stop the ship and deny us permission to leave. An Italian destroyer came alongside us and dropped anchor right on top of ours.

That was the first problem. But the more serious was the fact that our ship had no fuel at all, and we had not yet been informed where we would pick up the refugees. "Ma'apilim"—that is what we called the Jewish refugees traveling to Palestine. It means "those who climb up" in Hebrew. The word "aliyah" has a similar meaning, "to go up," and is the term used today for Jewish immigration to Israel. This is because Jews didn't just immigrate to Israel; rather they "climbed up" to the summit of their aspirations. They

76

climbed to the pinnacle of which they and their ancestors had been dreaming for two thousand years. Due to British interference, obviously, we would not be able to take on many refugees in Italy.

Thanks to Ada's ingenious help, we got down to refueling the ship. We were anchored close to the beach. Right there on the shore was an olive grove. In the darkness of the night we brought scores of tanker trailers into the area between the trees—two at a time, with their lights out. Four hose pipes were taken from the ship and into the grove. This is how we filled the tanks of the *President Warfield* without anyone noticing. Ada again used her influence with the Italian bureaucrats, and only then were we able to set sail. But only a few of the crew of American Jews, most of whom were alumni of the Zionist youth movement in the States and had volunteered for this covert operation, had any experience at sea. To me they were all dear friends who hailed from different cities around the United States, including New York, San Francisco, Atlanta, and Cincinnati.

We knew the British had been keeping track of the ship from the moment it left the United States. British intelligence, freshly discharged from the efforts imposed upon it by World War II, had been assigned the task of foiling our plans. Their intelligence network, the methods of spying, and the agents they engaged to uncover our plans were no less thorough than those they had applied against the German enemy: an irony of history. They tried to infiltrate every government ministry, every hotel, every port in which Aliyah Bet operated. They didn't hesitate to bully and threaten anyone they could into not helping us.

Even Shell, the large and important oil company that was then the largest supplier of fuel in the Mediterranean, was taking orders from the British Foreign Office. They were forbidden to supply fuel to any ship suspected

On board the Exodus: *faces of hope.*

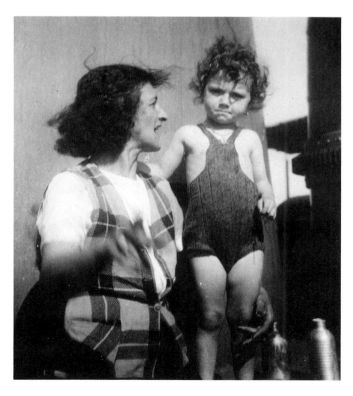

Three generations of immigrants on board the Exodus.

of being connected with the immigration effort to Palestine.

But we, too, were active. The Aliyah Bet representative in southern France, Shmaryahu Tzameret, was already waiting for us in Port de-Bouc. He received both a sympathetic ear and cooperation from French civil authorities. They identified with us in our struggle against the British and understood the human suffering of the Jewish refugees who wanted to get to their country. When we arrived in Port-de-Bouc, we immediately tied up to fuel-laden boats that were waiting for us. Before the British could intervene, we had more than enough fuel to cross the Mediterranean.

We were ready to take on our human cargo. Each of the ship's six decks had been divided into several "floors" with rows of wooden

bunks. Each bunk was six feet long and a foot and a half wide—so narrow that it was difficult to turn onto one's back. The rest of the conditions on the ship could be considered deluxe. We built large kitchens, even a sort of hospital. Both the internal and external communications systems were excellent.

The British were close behind us. One of their destroyers was anchored in the old port of Marseilles. The problem now was how to board the immigrants. Once again we were helped by the French authorities and French people, who hated the British no less than we did. They gave us authorization to take 1,300 Jewish refugees through France. We made another copy of the authorization papers in order to get 2,600 people out through two separate border checkpoints between Germany and France. Survivors of the Nazi carnage from Hungary, Romania, Poland, and other European countries conquered by the Third Reich left the refugee camps in Germany and came to southern France. After two or three days, we used the same documents to bring out a similar number of refugees.

We concentrated them in twelve camps along the beach, several hundred people in each camp. The Grand Armée camp was the biggest, with about 2,500 people. We organized them into sections of ten people each and platoons of three sections.

We maintained a low profile in order to avoid embarrassing the French authorities, who had asked that each refugee have an identity document and a visa. Ehud Avriel made a deal with the consul of a foreign country to give us thousands of visas in return for appropriate compensation. When the consul heard how many visas we wanted, he gave Ehud a rubber stamp and told him, "Do it yourself." Other colleagues went out onto the

Some of the 4,515 immigrants on their way to the Promised Land aboard the Exodus.

streets of Marseilles to round up photographers and bring them out to the camps. There they took passport photos of all the refugees and we were finally able to make up the documents.

One day before we were to sail, I went through all the camps in Marseilles to see my partners in the impending voyage. The meeting that shook me most was with six hundred children who had been put into one camp. They were orphans who had been found in the forests of Europe and sent to orphanages after their parents had become ash in the crematoria. Children ages three and four carried packs that were larger than they were. In those packs were photographs of families that no longer existed. I remember their faces, and I shall never forget their eyes. Their childlike smiles could not hide the sadness, the grief that flashed from their pupils; children who, despite their tender years, had been witness to some of the most horrific events mankind has chronicled. It was they who impressed upon me with an earth-shattering clarity the full importance of our struggle. We were saving the last remnants of an entire nation. This was what was left of six million Jews.

For the first time I began to feel that the whole British Empire did not possess enough ships or sufficient firepower in their cannons to stop us. As the hour for sailing neared, we moved from Port-de-Bouc to Port Sète. In an attempt to mislead British intelligence, we spread rumors and acted as if we would not leave for ten days.

We had arranged for 180 trucks to take the refugees to the ship. But on the day we boarded, there was a general strike by the truck drivers' union. Most of the drivers were members of the Communist Party—but they understood that our operation was in danger. Every truck carried a special travel permit so that the driver could not be accused of breaking the strike. At nine A.M. a British bomber appeared, making a reconnaissance flight over

the ship. But the trucks kept coming. A French border control official checked the identity documents. Sometimes he would ask questions such as "Why is this four-year-old child carrying a passport with the picture of a seventy-year-old man in it? What's going on here?" Then he would just look the other way.

When the refugees were loaded, we gathered up all the passports and burned them. Now there was no going back.

All of a sudden, totally out of the blue, the French authorities came along and told us that there was an order to stop the ship. They forbade us to sail.

Ike Aronovitch, two refugees, and I hurried out of the port to talk to the French governor. He was polite, but firm. "I'm sorry," he said, "but I have orders that we are not to let you sail." Meanwhile, more than four thousand refugees were roasting in the bowels of the ship in the hot July air. Some of the wooden bunks had broken. The people were tired. The French governor told us to move the ship to another place in the port where it would be more difficult for us to leave, but we refused. French police then boarded the ship to ensure that we would not sail. An American priest named John Grauel, who traveled with us, kept the French busy, drinking cognac with them.

Ready to sail but unable to move, we felt that we had failed. At nine P.M. I was called off the ship to a restaurant on the beach just outside the port. A phone call from Shaul Avigur awaited me:

"Shalom, Yossi."

"Shalom, Shaul."

"Can you hear me well?"

"I hear you fine."

"[Ernest] Bevin [the British Foreign Minister] has come to Paris especially from London to convince the French to stop the ship. Daniel Meyer told Venia that we should get the hell out of here, because in the morning we are going to be arrested. We have to do everything on our own."

Venia Pomerantz was Shaul's assistant in Paris. He was liaison officer to Minister of the Interior Édouard Depreux, Minister of Labor Daniel Mayer, and Léon Blum. Venia believed that the French security services would allow us to sail, provided we decided to do so without delay. I returned to the ship. We found a French navigator who could get the *Exodus* out of port. He agreed to come at two A.M., but it was well past three A.M. with the fishing boats already going out and no navigator in sight. We had promised a sum of money that would last him the rest of his life, but hundreds of thousands of dollars were worthless when the fate of our people was in the balance. In the meantime we had loosened five of the ropes that tied the ship to the dock. There was one rope left. Captain Ike made ready to sail with the aid of First Mate William (Bill) Bernstein, and Chief Officer Bernie Marks, both American Jews.

Dawn was breaking. We decided to go without the navigator. At four A.M. I gave the order to sail. Bill Bernstein cut the last rope with an ax. He would be killed by the British a few days later.

We turned on the engines, but the ship didn't move. One of the officers jumped overboard and found the problem. The ship's propeller was tangled in a steel cable. We had no divers to repair it and morning was coming. We decided to try and tear the cable, praying that no damage would come to the propeller. The whole of the upper deck, which was of wood, shuddered. For half an hour we switched the engines from forward to reverse, back and forth, until we heard a dull thud. The cable had broken and the ship was moving. The ship bumped and scraped along the sides of the docks. We didn't have a navigator; our exit from the port under our own steam was a work of art. It was only later that I heard that Léon Blum had written an article

On board the Exodus.

in Paris under the headline "Le Miracle" in which he described how inexplicable it was that a ship holding 4,500 people had sailed with no navigator.

One can now understand why we were so frustrated when, just as we were leaving the port, we hit the sandbank. That is where the second miracle took place.

When we finally got out to sea, we felt as though all the difficulties and disappointments of the last weeks had been worthwhile. The sea was calm, the weather balmy. It was a nice way to start our voyage to the Promised Land.

A British destroyer stuck to us like a shadow from the moment we left port, staying at a distance of approximately two miles. On one occasion the British came up close to us and asked, "Are you carrying illegal immi-

July 18, 1947: The Exodus surrenders after being attacked by British ships.

The Exodus *is stopped by the British: The toll is 3 killed, 200 wounded.*

grants to Palestine?" We did not reply. They would find out for themselves in the coming days.

During the night between July 11 and 12, another destroyer joined the first one. The British destroyers would continue to multiply like wasps. Reconnaissance planes also joined the destroyers. They flew over our ship at low altitude, making repeated sorties. Once in a while one of these destroyers would come within about 325 feet of us, trying to get a closer look.

Whenever we had the chance, we would visit with our passengers. They were young

people from Russia, Poland, and Czechoslovakia who had been in displaced persons camps in Germany from the end of the war; "elderly" religious people from Hungary, Lithuania, and Romania; and Jews from Holland, France, Belgium, and Italy. Their most remarkable characteristic was their peace of mind. Even though conditions were cramped and we were being hounded by destroyers, there was a silence and tranquillity that could only be ascribed to people at peace with themselves and their goals. It is difficult to think of a greater contrast than that between the expressions on the faces of the refugees and the threatening look of the British destroyers surrounding us.

"When we saw the coast of Europe disappearing in the distance," one refugee later told me, "a group of us stood up and said that Europe had once been our home, but after all that Europe has done to us, we hoped never to set foot on its soil again."

Of all the immigrant ships I commanded, the *Exodus* had the finest crew. Its members were dedicated people, never distracted by other concerns and totally committed to our mission. Under the command of Captain Ike Aronovitch, a member of the Palmach's naval unit, the crew was composed of two sections: the technical group, consisting of young American volunteers who joined us out of idealism with no thought of money, and the remaining staff, made up of Palestinian Jews of the Haganah. One of the Americans would die on board the ship in our struggle with the British; six others would be killed during the War of Independence.

The Haganah members included Micha Perry, who took care of the refugees; Azriel Einav, our outstanding communications officer; Danny Katznelson, from Kibbutz Kfar Menachem, responsible for the food; and Sima, from Kibbutz Afikim, who took care of the children and handled our medical supplies.

During our third night at sea, two babies were born on the ship. We were told there were other women on board who were about to give birth. When daylight came, a storm broke out. At least half the passengers became seasick. The members of the crew vacated their own cabins to make them available for the sick and the elderly.

The British warships escorting us were joined by the *Ajax,* the cruiser that, during the war, had sunk the famous German warship *Graf Spee* off Montevideo. She transmitted a message to us: "If you are carrying immigrants, you are acting illegally. We will imprison you as soon as you reach territorial waters." Some of our crew members wanted to reply, "This ship is not the *Graf Spee.*" But we overcame this impulse and simply answered: "We received your message. Thank you."

Not until 1987 was I at last allowed to read the exchange of secret cables relating to the *Exodus* kept in the British Admiralty archives in London. The confidential telegram sent to the *Ajax* on the afternoon of July 14, 1947, by the commander of the British Navy in the Mediterranean read:

"1. Now that *Warfield* is well clear of Malta you should start the verbal softening up process on her, having first asked where she is bound.

"2. The softening should be on the lines that passengers will not be allowed to land in Palestine, that no one wishes passengers any harm but it is the duty of the Royal Navy to see that the law is carried out and H.M. Ships will, if necessary, use overwhelming force to carry out this duty and that resistance is useless and can only lead to injury.

"3. This should be passed in as many European languages as you have available."

The message ended with a mysterious order: "Nothing is to be said about the destination of the passengers after the ship has been seized."

This is how the Admiralty in London prepared the trap. The refugees were forbidden to know that the British intended to take them back to Europe. The British must have suspected that this would only increase their resistance.

On the fourth day another child was born on the ship, a boy. But the mother, in spite of good medical treatment, hemorrhaged and died. The bereaved father stood sadly beside his new son. It was a heart-rending moment. I could not stop thinking of the cruel irony of this young woman, who had gone through all kinds of hell in order to come to Eretz Yis-

The Exodus *following its arrival in Haifa on July 18, 1947.*

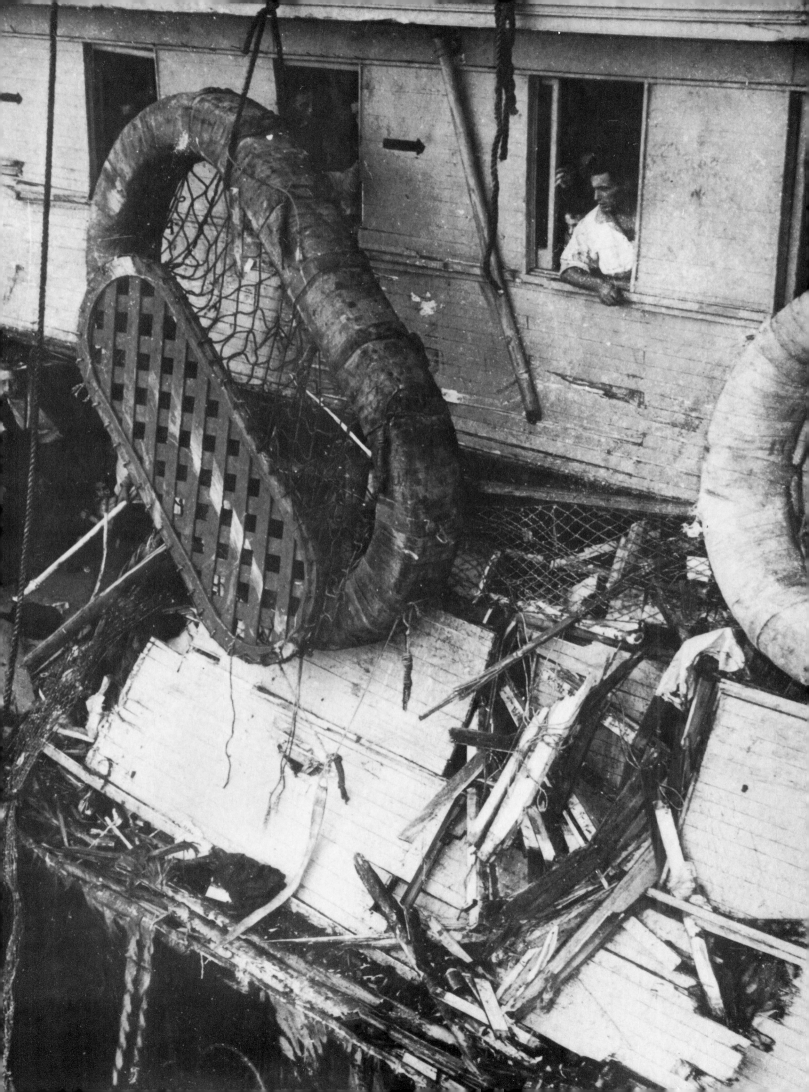

rael, only to meet her death just short of its gates.

This was our first casualty on the voyage of the *Exodus*. We put a metal chain around the woman's legs, wrapped her body in a blue and white flag, and formed a guard of honor. We stood at attention as the body was slowly lowered into the sea.

Our ship had an excellent communications system operated by Azriel Enav. We regularly exchanged coded messages with our clandestine headquarters in Palestine. When necessary we also had direct contact with our European command post in Paris.

On July 13 they asked us: "What is the exact number of passengers you are carrying—men, women, and children? How many foreign crewmen are there? How many lifeboats and what is their condition?"

On July 14 we replied: "We are carrying 4,515. Men: 1,561; women: 1,282; children: 655; adolescents: 1,017; crew: 36."

The same day we requested the high command to give us a Hebrew name for the ship. We gave every ship in our phantom fleet a symbolic name, linked to our struggle against the British for the establishment of our state and the running of their blockade along the shores of Palestine.

We received the reply two days later, on July 16: "Your name in English is *'Exodus 1947'* and in Hebrew *'Yetziat Europa 5707.'* The names must appear together."

We were making headway at speeds of between eleven and fourteen knots. Through thirty loudspeakers scattered throughout the ship, we would broadcast news six times a day. The refugees organized and published a daily newspaper in several languages, including articles as well as poetry. But from the outset we were also prepared for the war at sea, which the British had declared on us. Yes, this was a real war. And now, around the *Exodus,* it was an open war. It was clear to us that there was no way of averting a confronta-

tion with the British. The destroyers, whose numbers grew almost daily, were a constant reminder of this. We made all the necessary preparations to greet the British. We closed off all the passageways with screens. We prepared an "arsenal": piles of canned food, screws, nails, wooden planks, potatoes.

Every day the refugees practiced repelling the British the moment they would try to board the *Exodus.* We conducted manuevers and exercises. At the sound of the ship's horn, everyone was to man his station. We strung barbed wire around the bridge. We even installed a spare wheel on a lower deck, just in case we should lose control of the bridge.

When we neared the Egyptian coast around Port Said, we were escorted by a whole flotilla of warships: five destroyers and one cruiser. The ships belonged to the Palestine patrol, the special British naval force to prevent Jewish immigration. We were sailing from south to north, but on a very different route than that taken by our forefathers on their Exodus from Egypt thousands of years ago. Not through the Sinai Desert this time, but along the coast, passing by Al-Arish and Gaza to Tel Aviv. We did not travel at full speed, so as not to let the British know how fast we could go. We had two British ships on either side of us, plus one in front and one behind.

Through our communications system, we finalized our plan with the Haganah in Eretz Yisrael. As we neared Tel Aviv, we planned to increase speed to full power and then suddenly stop the engines. The British would overshoot us before they realized what was happening. We would then make a ninety-degree turn toward the Tel Aviv shore and at our full speed of eighteen knots run the ship up onto the beach. We estimated it would take us ten to fifteen minutes to reach the shore, during which time two battalions of the Palmach would bar the British police from the beach and wait for us. We would disembark as many passengers as possible. We had a good chance because the ship had been built for river travel and had a very flat keel, which would enable us to get very close to the beach. The British destroyers, on the other hand, could not get so close without running on a sandbank.

It was a good plan—even daring. But the British may have broken our transmission codes. Years later I found in the archives documents indicating that the British, precisely because of this suspicion, decided to attack our ship on the high seas, outside of territorial waters.

On July 17, still on the open sea, the commander of the British war fleet on the deck of the destroyer H.M.S. *Chequers* posted the orders "for the boarding and arrest of the *President Warfield*." The document was classified as "secret—to be destroyed by fire when complied with." The commander determined that the aim was "to ensure the quick arrest of the *President Warfield* by getting over the greatest number of men in the shortest possible time." He ordered: "All ships are to be fully darkened by 2100. At 1930, without further orders, ships will take their positions around the *Warfield* at a distance of one mile."

In the following hours, according to a previously arranged time table, each ship was to close in on the *Exodus* in turn, light up the ship with searchlights, and announce to her "the futility of resistance." Just before the takeover, the *Ajax* was "to take station between the *Warfield* and the beach as requisite."

Their goal was clearly to prevent the *Exodus* from getting near the shores of Palestine at any price. And then the order would be given to gain control of the ship:

"The boarding position should be near *Warfield*'s wheelhouse . . . each ship should endeavor to put three complete boarding parties," onto the deck of the *President Warfield*.

"Lt. MacPherson, Royal Navy H.M.S. *Chieftain,* will command the boarding parties. Each group is to make contact with him and follow his orders.

"It is intended that the wheelhouse should be secured first and as quickly as possible in order to control the ship's course.

"The next objective should be to clear the top and boat decks and establish some sort of citadel."

Only then, "a strong party should be sent, first, to take charge of the steering engine and, secondly, to gain control of the engine room."

Attached to the orders of this operation were sketches of the *President Warfield* made in 1944 in order to "assist boarding parties to find the best route to gain control of her." The unit commander, Naval Lieutenant Mac-Pherson, was given "the Gunner."

The commander of the flotilla decided that "the *Ajax* is requested to do all she can to ride *President Warfield* away from the beach should the need arise."

Even the role of the destroyer *Cardigan Bay* was outlined in detail:

"1. Recovery of any of the Boarding Party who may fall into the sea.

"2. Recovery of any Jews who attempt to swim from the ship to shore."

The British orders for the operation covered a mere two pages, pages that would ignite a flame by the light of which the *Exodus* would shine for generations to come.

At that time we were unaware of the details of these secret preparations. All that we on the deck of the *Exodus* knew was that the British would do anything to prevent us from reaching the shores of Eretz Yisrael. For this reason we coordinated, through an exchange of messages with the command post in Palestine, the precise spot near Tel Aviv to which we would navigate the ship and where the Palmach forces would await us.

We decided that the beaching of the *Exodus* would take place on Friday, July 18, at nine in the morning.

In coordination with our high command,

we decided to broadcast a special message directly from the *Exodus* via the Haganah's clandestine radio transmitter in Palestine. On July 17 at ten P.M., the *Exodus* began a one-hour-long broadcast in Hebrew, English, and French: "Listen to the immigrant ship *Exodus,* a ship of the Hebrew Haganah, now nearing the shores of Eretz Yisrael. We are about sixty miles away, and each moment brings us closer to the coast we yearn for. Five British destroyers and one cruiser have us tightly encircled."

Thousands of Jews in Palestine stopped dead in their tracks when they heard the voices of their brothers and sisters from the ship. Within a short time, the contents of the transmission were on the front pages of the world's press. We told of the British chasing us, of the attempts to deny us fuel, of the British intervention in our departure from France. We called on the world to follow our ship's struggle. We invited the members of the U.N.'s Special Investigation Committee to board our ship to see its passengers for themselves. "We are not the last," we said in our broadcast. "No one will stop us from returning to our land and building our own state. Our 'Aliyah' will continue."

This is how a British officer on the destroyer *Chequers* described the events of July 17, in the hours just before the battle, in a report he submitted to his commander:

"0700. Joined company with *President Warfield* in position 11 miles north of Rosetta Mouth [Egyptian coast]. *Ajax* and *Childers* were in company in positions one mile on the port and starboard quarters respectively. Stationed *Chieftain* and *Charity* seven cables on the port and starboard beams respectively. *Chequers* took station astern. During daylight

Immigrants from the Exodus *on board prison ships chartered by the British for the voyage to Germany.*

90

hours ships were stationed so that the side on which they had made preparations to board was concealed from the *President Warfield.*

"0815. *Cardigan Bay* joined company and was stationed two miles ahead. *President Warfield*'s course and speed at this time was 102 degrees 12 knots. Her subsequent movements throughout the day were erratic but trended continuously towards the Palestine coast, and by 1800 it was clear that Boarding would probably take place in the vicinity of Gaza during the Middle Watch.

"0830–1130. All ships were given an opportunity to close *President Warfield* and examine her. Propaganda from Haifa [in the form of] Confidential Memoranda was passed at the same time.

"*Chequers* closed the *Ajax* and discussed the future employment of *Ajax* and her Boarding Parties over the loud hailer. . . .

"2100. Worrying tactics commenced and continued with hourly visitations throughout the night. Further propaganda was passed and *President Warfield* was clearly warned that she would be arrested if she attempted to enter territorial waters and efforts were made to persuade her to steer towards Haifa. The *President Warfield* engaged in flashing exercises with most ships. *Chequers* was treated to a fine vocal rendering of "The Yanks are Coming" by a Male Voice Choir. During *Chequers'* visit it was noted, however, that all the women and children had been massed on the top decks and the lower ones cleared for action. The prospect of achieving some measure of initial surprise therefore appeared good."

We were ten or twelve miles outside the territorial waters of Palestine. It was two A.M. on July 18. We hoped to reach the Tel Aviv coastline by morning.

And then, parallel to Gaza and a considerable distance beyond territorial waters, the British began their attack on us.

Two destroyers closed in on our sides. We sounded our siren. Nearly a thousand young

refugees came up on deck armed with sticks and canned food. The destroyers came at us in complete darkness. But the moment they approached us, they illuminated the *Exodus* with searchlights and warned us over loudspeakers: "You have entered territorial waters. Stop the ship. You are under arrest!"

Their bows lit the *Exodus* on both sides, and then they stepped up their speed in an attempt to cut us off. They ripped holes in the *Exodus.* But we increased our speed to its maximum and pushed them aside. The British fired machine guns at the decks. In the first volley, one refugee was killed and forty to fifty others were wounded.

Two more destroyers immediately appeared, employing the same tactics, their bows ramming the *Exodus.* Young children and boys in their teens stood on deck through the night throwing cans of food, screws, and nails at the British sailors trying to clamber from their vessels onto the *Exodus.* Each time a destroyer rammed us, the British threw gas and smoke bombs onto the *Exodus* while, at the same time, their boarding parties tried to board our ship. This battle at sea in the dark of night lives on in my mind as no less cruel and bloody—perhaps even more so—than any clashes we have witnessed, before or since, in the wars we have been called on to fight.

This is how the start of the battle is described in the confidential documents of the destroyer H.M.S. *Chequers:* At 1:52 A.M. the *Chequers* was given the order to prepare to seize the ship. But almost another hour passed (2:44 A.M.) before the order was issued to begin the operation.

"*Chieftain* and *Childers* closed to board from the starboard and port sides respectively but at the critical moment *President Warfield* made a large decrease in speed (probably for-

British troops forcibly disembarking immigrants from the Exodus.

tuitously) causing *Childers* to overshoot so that a second approach had to be made and the initial boarding was not synchronised. By this time the alarm was raised in *President Warfield* who increased speed to about 13 knots and commenced violent alterations of course. She was subsequently almost continuously under helm throughout the boarding operations until 0500, except for the short period when [the] *Childers* Boarding Party had control of the steering from the wheelhouse before the Jews changed to after steering. The greater manoeuvreability of *President Warfield* and the skill with which she was handled made it extremely difficult for Destroyers to get alongside, and once there to remain for long.

"Many alongsides were made, but men got across in small numbers only and in the face of fierce opposition. Between 0300 and 0330 *Childers* got across three officers and 20 men. She then reported that her Boarding Platform had collapsed and that she was damaged, and *Charity* took her place. *Charity* succeeded in getting over one officer and four men before she also reported herself damaged and unfit for further boarding."

From the other side of the *Exodus,* the *Chieftain* was able to get three officers and six men on board. This was a desperate battle that defies description. We sprayed heavy fuel at the British. Our people tried to fend them off with poles and push them into the water. Our youngsters hurled all the food we had on board at them. We succeeded in throwing some of the gas bombs back onto the decks of the destroyers.

Suddenly I heard the shouts of a child as he ran from the lower deck to the upper deck. The boy screamed as he sped along the upper deck and reached the body of a youngster who had been killed. It was his thirteen-year-old brother. (I subsequently learned that his name was Hirsch Yakabovitch.) They were two orphans. He had suddenly gotten the feeling that something had happened to his brother. And so it had.

From the force of the impact of the British ships hitting us, some of our rafts fell onto the decks of the destroyers and damaged them. The British seized control of our bridge, the wheel, and the navigating equipment. Water began leaking into the ship. Panic reigned. The British finally succeeded in infiltrating a small group into the wheelhouse on the bridge—it was there that they killed Bill Bernstein. We did not let the British out of the wheelhouse. We disconnected the main wheel. It was a face-to-face battle on the upper deck, the lower deck, and in the wheelhouse.

Just in time we retreated to the stern of the ship. In Italy we had prepared for the possibility of having to navigate the ship by using a wheel we had installed in the stern. But our compass was a simple one and it was difficult to navigate. We sailed at full speed, zigzagging all the time. We wove our way in and out between the destroyers. This is how we made our way northward toward the lights of Jaffa and Tel Aviv. The shores of our land were so close, and yet we could not reach them.

The crying and screaming of the refugees on board ship increased. The ship began to perilously fill with water; 2,500 people sat below decks and the water had already reached their knees. To get their minds off the precarious situation and improve morale, we armed the refugees with buckets and instructed them to start baling out as much water as possible.

As dawn broke, the captains of the destroyers described the drama to the commander of their flotilla in a series of short messages couched in routine military jargon:

"0200: Ready to board the *Warfield.*

"0242: Preparing to board now.

"0317: Only 10 men boarded the ship. Heavy resistance.

"0345: 40 men now on her deck. Still impossible [for the destroyers] to get close

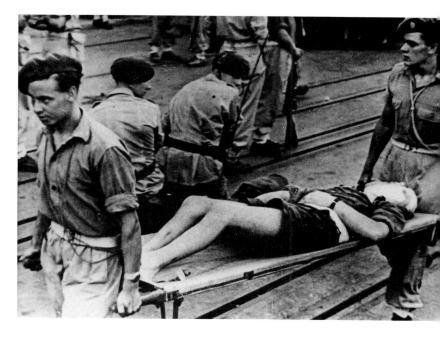

The wounded on the Exodus *are evacuated by British troops.*

enough to the ship for a long enough time, due to wild changes in direction.

"0445: Another six have boarded her deck. *President Warfield* is using gas.

"0530: The captain [of the *Warfield*] is now cooperating and ready to sail to Haifa. The ship has requested medical aid for 20 wounded Jews."

The commander of the destroyers flotilla later wrote in a confidential report of August 10, 1947:

"I am extremely doubtful whether a foothold would ever have been established in the *President Warfield* had boarding platforms not been constructed in Destroyers. Credit for this suggestion belongs to *Childers*. It is evident that *President Warfield* had made effective preparations to resist any boarding on her foc'sle, quarterdeck and promenade decks and

The disembarkation in Hamburg of the immigrants from the Exodus: *a British soldier carrying the meager baggage of an exhausted woman.*

had massed her women and children on the top decks in consequence. . . . [T]he platforms gave the initial boarders some measure of surprise which enabled them to get to the wheelhouse fairly quickly. This established a stronghold in the early stages and formed a rallying point for subsequent parties. If this had not been the case it seems certain that the small parties that got across at each alongside would have been overwhelmed individually as

in fact occurred to *Chequers* party. Indeed up to 0515 both *Chieftain* and myself were under the impression that this had probably been occurring.

". . . I wish to emphasize the very fine way in which the Commanding Officers handled their ships. The difficulty of trying to get alongside a ship more maneourveable [sic] than yourself which is taking continuous and violent avoiding action in the dark can well be imagined. Once there, it was impossible to remain for anything but a very short time beacuse [sic] of (a) the swell, (b) the heavy construction of *President Warfield,* (c) the fact that the Boarding platforms were of necessity at the pivoting point of the ship, and (d) the anti-boarding measures taken against the ships themselves. Under the circumstances the damage done to . . . ships was unavoidable and might have been a great deal worse had the ships been in less experienced hands.

"Though the wind, sea and swell decreased after sunset, they were estimated at wind force 3 and sea and swell 23 when Boarding started; the risk of serious damage was accepted in view of the importance of preventing this ship making the Palestine Coast. . . . In addition it has always been understood that widespread disorders of a very serious nature will follow a landing in the Tel Aviv area."

Reading these secret British reports forty years later confirms our feeling at the time; we, the refugee ship *Exodus,* had gotten the better of the mighty British Navy.

A British captain described the antiboarding measures taken against his crewmen:

"*Missiles.* The hail of missiles was heavier and more effective than ever met before. The objects used ranged from the dropping of large skid rafts and lifeboats on the destroyers' decks to iron scaffolding poles 12 feet x 2 inches, buckets, crow bars, nuts, bolts, and all manner of food, including whole cases, and tins of all descriptions.

"*Smoke.* Aircraft[/]ship distress signals in

large cannisters of American originard [sic] special smoke cannisters were ignited and thrown on board ships, and used against the Boarding Party in the wheelhouse of *President Warfield*. These burnt with an intense flame giving out a thick yellow smoke. This smoke caused considerable embarrassment to Boarding Parties and Bridge personnel.

"*Tear Smoke*. Quite a large number of tear smoke grenades similar to type 91 were thrown on board ships. It is not known whether they were part of *President Warfield*'s equipment or taken off Boarding Parties. In the case of *Chequers* they were used most effectively against the Bridge personnel.

"*Steam Jet*. Examination of this system after the immigrants had disembarked show it to consist of a continuous steam pipe the full length of the ship both sides and outboard of everything at the height of a destroyer's foc'sle. There were holes in this pipe at two foot intervals throughout its length through which steam issued. It was ineffective against Boarding Parties due to insufficient pressure and the height at which Boarding Parties went over, but the heat of the steam could just be felt by ratings working on *Chieftain*'s foxle [sic].

"*Oil Fuel Jet*. This system was fitted on the starboard side only and used against *Chieftain*. Subsequent examination showed it to consist of an oil fuel supply pipe led up from below to the Boat Deck with a "Y" piece at the top from which two canvas hoses were led. These were connected to 12 foot scaffolding poles lashed to the guard rails on the Boat Deck and directed downwards on to the Boarding Destroyer. Considerable quantity of oil was pumped on to *Chieftain* from the bows to the Flag Deck, and made the Decks and Boarding Platforms extremely difficult to work on. Attempts were made by the Jews to fire this oil by throwing over sea boots filled with oily waste and ignited, suitcases filled with wood shaving and ignited and by distress flares. Fire was averted by prompt action in ditching these objects.

"*Weapons*. The extent of the weapons used against the Boarding Parties on *President Warfield* can best be guaged [sic] by reading the Boarding Officers' reports. Apart from missiles they included the use of horsewhips, oars, sticks, axes and coshes [blackjacks]. . . ."

The ship's surgeon, Dr. Cohen from England, came to tell me that we had forty wounded and it was imperative that they be given blood transfusions. But we had no plasma, and if they did not receive proper treatment, there was a danger that six or seven could die.

This was the last straw. I had not been chosen to command the *Exodus* to deliver dead corpses. No man had the moral right to let the wounded die. This was not a suicide ship but a human cargo of thousands who had been saved from gas chambers and were coming to build a new life in their own land. We told one of the British officers that he should inform his commander that we had many wounded, and we stopped the ship.

At first they were wary of getting too close to us. Then slowly, like a pack of wolves, the British destroyers surrounded us, closing in suspiciously with their bows aimed at us. It was a strange sight off the sunlit coast between Tel Aviv and Haifa. The descendants of the revered and renowned Lord Nelson, hero of the sea battles at Trafalgar and Abu Kir, had won a signal victory against a hopeless refugee ship!

A surgeon lieutenant of the Royal Navy, D. C. S. Beit, a doctor on the destroyer *Chequers*, came aboard onto the fuel-drenched and blood-stained deck. He turned pale as a ghost when he saw the children lying there wounded. This is the report he later wrote:

"At approximately 0545 on 18th July, 1947, I boarded the *President Warfield*. . . . My first act was to proceed to the Hospital aft, and try and ascertain the general position. I found one youth of about 16 very nearly dead with a head injury of some kind, which the Jewish Doctor told me was a gunshot wound. I administered a maximum dose of strychnine as a stimulant, but the boy died within about 30 minutes. There was rather a hysterical scene with his younger brother, and I did not think it wise to start tampering with the body in order to verify the cause of death. There was one other serious head injury in the Sick Bay, who was moribund, and to whom I administered strychnine at intervals until my supply ran out, and whose condition improved a little, but who remained in a moribund state all day. Other serious cases in the Sick Bay included a broken jaw, a head injury with bullet wound of abdomen, and a through and through bullet wound of the wrist. . . .

"I was then taken round the ship by a Hospital Attendant, an American named Offey(?) who, though resentful of British methods, and ignoring the fact that the Jews were wielding axes and other lethal weapons and would have done any damage they could, was very cooperative and helpful. He was an immigrant, working his passage, to the land where he had been told there were hundreds of miles of country, waiting developement [sic]. He saw no reason why he, and others, shoul[d] not go and develop it. Any arguments put forward against unrestricted immigration he dismissed as 'British Boloney.'"

"He showed me more casualties, turned in in [sic] cabins of the upper deck, including the First Mate of the ship, an American, suffering from a fracture of the base of his skull, with very definite brain stem damage. I also saw a bullet wound of the right loin, one of

Immigrants from the Exodus *confined to the* Runnymede Park, *a deportation ship equipped with cages, anchored off Port-de-Bouc, pending its departure for Germany.*

98

the lower abdomen and a mild one of the left chest and arm, all in youths of 18 or so. There was also the usual assortment of mild head injuries and cuts. We went down below on to the "messdecks," through a mass of humanity, mostly asleep on top of all its worldly possessions, and he told me of the number of cases of chronic disease on board, as epilepsy, cardiac failure of various types, tuberculosis, diabetics, etc. . . .

"The conditions below decks were not nearly as bad as I expected. They were very overcrowded, but reasonably clean, as also were the people themselves, especially the children, of whom there were about 1000 aboard. This surprised me, as the sanitary equipment did not appear to have been supplemented very much, and the ship was not designed to carry 5000.

"Having reviewed the situation as a whole, I asked Lieutenant MacPherson to make a signal to say that there were about 200 cases in need of proper nursing care. This was only a very rough estimate, and I still have no idea how correct it was. . . .

"The existing medical organisation of the ship appeared to be designed to cope with casualties. . . . Three Jewish Doctors presided, one of whom spoke good English, and seemed efficient, though the situation was really too much for him. . . .

"The English speaking Doctor, however, was a great help. He had been doing most of the treatment of medical cases during the voyage, and he supplied us with a list of some 35 severe cases which he had under his care. Also he had seen about 75 women in the last month of preg[n]ancy, some with toxaemias. We made a further signal about this. But he said that he was convinced there were many more cases below who had not come to him, and the number he gave us, added to about 30 casualties whom we saw, gave about 140 needing some sort of hospitalization. I consider it very likely that a further 60 could have been found below on the messdecks, to make my original estimate of 200 fairly accurate.

"In general, we were sorry not to have been able to do more, but heroic measures on severe head injuries are not worth while. . . . Our own casualties were three. . . . None of these were very severe. . . .

"I was impressed by the damage done by our men to the Jews on the Upper Deck of the ship. These included many youths of sixteen or eighteen, who had been wielding axes and knives on the ends of pieces of rope. I am told that some of them were armed with American Automatic Pistols. Clearly, they were prepared to kill if they got the chance, but when wounded, especially if with bullets, they were full of whines and injured innocence. All our sailors, having used force very successfully to establish control, were extremely helpful in tending the wounded. I know of one who became involved in a slight skirmish after I came aboard, who knocked his opponent down and rendered him useless for further combat, and then proceeded immediately to administer first aid from the pack he was carrying. I have great admiration for all of them."

In a secret letter dated September 15, 1947, the commander of the British Navy in the Mediterranean wrote to the British Navy high command in London:

"This was by far the most difficult and dangerous boarding so far carried out by the Palestine Patrol. It would have failed but for the determination and the excellent ship-handling displayed by all Commanding Officers; the considerable damage sustained by destroyers might well have been much greater."

During the whole two-and-a-half-hour battle, we reported by radio to our high command in Palestine. We kept them updated, and corrected reports as the fog of battle over the *Exodus* cleared:

"July 18, 1947:

"0516: Outside territorial waters, approximately 25 miles from shore. About 6 destroyers have attacked us. The battle has been going on for more than two and a half hours. We have 10 prisoners, some of them wounded seriously. We have three dead, two of them children, about 20 wounded from bullets, some of them critically. We are negotiating with the British prisoners. All the weapons we captured have been thrown into the sea. A destroyer is now to take the wounded.

"0518: It must be mentioned that the spirit of our people is firm. The ship has been badly damaged. The whole wooden structure has been shattered. Water has leaked into the engine room. The bridge is not in our hand. I am steering with the spare wheel from the keel of the ship. We are in control of the ship. We are headed for Haifa. Destroyers escort us on all sides. Planes are hovering overhead. We have scores of badly wounded, still negotiating with the prisoners. Correction: We are holding 30 British prisoners, all of them concentrated on the bridge. We are in control of the ship.

"0525: There is danger of our sinking. The ship has sprung a leak. We continue at full speed towards Haifa where we will disembark wounded. We still have the prisoners. I repeat recent developments. We are still in control of the vessel. We continue towards Haifa. The wooden structure has been destroyed. The ship is taking water. We are continuing at full speed toward Haifa in order to disembark the wounded. Stay tuned. We are continuing with our broadcasts."

"0730: You are listening to the immigrant ship *Exodus*. We continue with our broadcast. Latest summary of casualties: One dead, 5 dying. 15–20 in critical condition, 80–100 suffering from light wounds.

"1200: We have managed to overcome the water leaks. The pumps are working at full power. We are making for Haifa at full speed. Safety condition of the vessel is reasonable. We expect to arrive in Haifa at 1500 Palestine

1947: concentration camp in Cyprus.

time. No change in the condition of the wounded. We are in good spirits, our will is strong.

"1250: You are listening to the immigrant ship *Exodus*. I continue with the information. We will arrive in Haifa in an hour and a half. In the distance, we can see Carmel mountains. The condition of the wounded is unchanged. If treatment is not administered as fast as humanly possible, we may lose some people. Those in an extremely critical condition are dying."

All in all, three people died in this battle with the British. The third victim was also a refugee, Mordechai Bomstein. It must be remembered that the reports referred to above were sent during the heat of battle.

We sailed into the port of Haifa according to our agreement with the British. We came into port with a battered ship, but with people whose spirits remained unbroken. We had done the best we could. We had tried to resist, that was the most we could do. We could no longer endanger the lives of those few who had survived where millions had perished. *Exodus* had already lost three people and scores of wounded. We had broken through the blockade imposed on us in Europe and here, on the shores of Palestine, we had brought our problem into the limelight, before the whole world.

But the tortured route of the *Exodus* did not end that afternoon. In Haifa, the British transferred the refugees to three prison ships and prepared to expel them.

Some of us, members of the Haganah, and the American crew members, hid in places on the ship that we had prepared in advance. Once the refugees left, our Haganah comrades helped us off the ship and out of Haifa. It was important to rescue the crew, because other immigrant ships awaited us. The *Pan York* was awaiting me personally in Marseilles.

But the British Empire had decided to play a cynical game with the poor refugees. Usually, once the British had stopped one of our immigrant ships, they would transfer the passengers to prison camps on the island of Cyprus. This time, however, Foreign Minister Ernest Bevin, who was rabidly opposed to Jewish immigration, and the founding of an independent Jewish state in Palestine, decided to teach the *Exodus* passengers a lesson. He gave orders to return them to Europe, to their point of departure, Port-de-Bouc. In so doing, Bevin turned the *Exodus* into an international symbol. Public opinion, influenced by the world's press, followed the struggles of the *Exodus* refugees day by day. Behind the wire netting, in the cages of the expulsion ships, the British Government had placed its prestige on the *Exodus.*

For three weeks, in the summer heat of July and August, the three ships lay anchored in Port-de-Bouc. The British wanted the refugees to leave the ships. But the French Government announced it would accept them only if they disembarked voluntarily, and the refugees refused to get off, except for two elderly people who were sick. "We will only disembark in Eretz Yisrael," they sang over and over again.

Finally, Bevin had no choice but to bring this theater of the absurd to its climax. He ordered the ships to sail to British-controlled Hamburg, in occupied Germany—the same Germany from which the refugees had been saved. There they would be taken off by force. Many were beaten and could no longer stand on their feet. Even the most callous-hearted would have been horrified when the refugees were returned to concentration camps, this time under the British and on German soil.

The British thought they were dealing with weaklings. But the old people, the children, the sick were all of one mind—to get to Eretz

A concentration camp reserved by the British for illegal Jewish immigrants (Cyprus, August 1947).

Yisrael. This was an irresistible force. *Exodus* became a symbol not because of us but because of the British. Bevin thought he was terminating Jewish immigration to Israel by punishing the *Exodus*. Instead, he instilled in us a renewed fighting spirit. Everything the Haganah had promised, it fulfilled. All immigrants of the *Exodus* would arrive in Israel. Within a few months, everyone did get there. Some arrived as legal immigrants to the state which had just been born.

The crew of the *Exodus* had another trip, this time bringing more than fifteen thousand refugees at once, to the shores of Eretz Yisrael aboard the *Pan York* and the *Pan Crescent*. I was appointed commander of the flotilla that set out at the end of December 1947 from the port of Burgas in Bulgaria through the Dardanelles to Palestine. British destroyers again awaited us in the Mediterranean. Our will to fight, as well as self-sacrifice, sophistication, and determination—all were displayed in an exemplary fashion by the *Exodus*. These are after all the same foundations upon which the State of Israel has been based during the first forty years of her existence.

Exodus: The Aftermath

THE CRUEL VOYAGE of the *Exodus* lasted eight weeks—until the British finally succeeded in forcing the refugees back to German soil, on the deportation ship *Ocean Vigour*. More than any other Haganah operation, the journey of these unfortunate refugees attracted the world's attention to the Jewish dilemma. This human story of the British Navy's battle against refugee women and children received daily coverage in the international newspapers and radio.

This is how United Press recorded the end of the passengers' arrival in Hamburg on September 8, 1947:

"British troops today landed 1,400 screaming, kicking, and weeping Jewish refugees from the transport *Ocean Vigour,* using physical force to compel recalcitrants to set foot on German soil. Truncheons were employed sparingly.

"The unloading of the *Ocean Vigour* was the first phase of the debarkation of some 4,300 Jews who had sought to go to Palestine aboard the blockade runner *Exodus 1947.* . . .

"The trouble began when about half the refugees aboard the ship had debarked. State-helmeted British troops entered the holds and dragged or carried Jews up the pier.

"One Jew was stunned by a truncheon blow, and a number appear to have engaged in fisticuffs with the troops. About one in seven of the *Ocean Vigour*'s passengers had to be removed with some degree of physical pressure. 'Dirty fascists!' some of the refugees screamed at the British soldiers as they were hustled ashore.

"The refugees were packed aboard a train and taken to the Poppendorf displaced persons camp eight miles from Lübeck. They shouted, 'Auschwitz,' 'Belsen,' 'Maidanek'—the names of infamous Nazi extermination camps—and hurled food at the troops as their train rolled away."

The scene on the deck of the *Ocean Vigour* was repeated with the refugees who boarded the second deportation ship, the *Empire Royal.*

Hamburg: heading for British concentration camps.

The end of the journey: passengers from the Exodus behind the barbed wire of British camps in Germany (Am Stau, near Lübeck).

The last stage of the voyage of torment of the *Exodus* refugees, who were forced off the deportation ship *Runnymede Park*, was described that day by the Associated Press as follows:

"British troops today carried scores of bloody, battered Jews out of the hold of the transport *Runnymede Park* after turning fire hoses on the defiant refugees and beating them into submission with rubber clubs and wooden billies.

"The British Army reported casualties as 17 Jewish men injured, 7 Jewish women injured, 4 Jewish women hospitalized because of hysteria, and 3 British soldiers injured. Troops of the Sixth Airborne Division—the famous Red Devils—[as well as] Sherwood Foresters and military police fought their way into the holds of the *Runnymede Park* when the Jews defied orders to disembark. They played steams from high pressure fire hoses on the refugees and then entered the holds equipped with steel helmets, wooden billies and rubber truncheons made from automobile tyres.

"A fierce battle in the hold of the ship was fought out of the view of correspondents crowded at the pier.

"The Jews fought with such improvised weapons as broken bottles and sticks tipped with barbed wire and razor blades.

"Five groups of troops were dispatched into the ship. It took them more than an hour to quell the angered refugees.

"Then the troops formed into five-men crews and began to pass the battered refugees up from the hold and down the gangplank to German soil.

"The refugees, blood streaming from their heads and wounds on their necks, arms, and

At the camp of Am Stau, only 300 prisoners out of a total of 1,400 are allowed to recover their meager baggage.

bodies, were carted off unceremoniously in a display which made the unloading of the transport *Ocean Vigour* yesterday resemble a tea party. Defying the order to disembark, the Jews had clustered together in the holds, singing Jewish hymns and anthems. The moment the stream of water was cut off, the voices of the Jews were heard in the mournful chorus of an ancient Hebrew hymn.

"A Jewish woman shouted: 'Go ahead, beat us. Shoot us. Hitler did the same thing. You are no different.' The only benefit from using the water cannon was forcing Jewish women and some Jewish men who were caring for their children, to come out of their places of hiding on board the ship. Even after the refugees were placed on board the trains, the violence did not cease."

Only on Tuesday, September 9, was the British Navy commander in Hamburg able to notify London: "the last Jews from the *Exodus* have been put ashore."

Golda Myerson (later changed to Meir) expressed her dismay over the *Exodus* affair by saying, "If I live to be one hundred, the terrible sight of hundreds of British soldiers, in full gear, carrying and using clubs, pistols, and grenades against the miserable refugees on the deck of the *Exodus,* including four hundred pregnant women who were resolved to give birth in Eretz Yisrael, can never be erased from my eyes. I will also never be able to forget the revulsion that arose in me when I heard that they indeed would return these people, like animals in metal cages, to the displacement camps in that very country which symbolized the graveyard of European Jewry."

These shocking descriptions reinforced the resolve of Jews, both in Palestine and abroad, to fight the British with whatever means possible. Many enlisted in the underground, either in the Haganah or the more radical Irgun or Stern groups. Sympathetic functionaries in the French Government looked the other way at their activities; some even offered outright assistance.

But there was a limit to that cooperation, and it ceased in September 1947, when police arrested fourteen people in France and charged them with plotting to drop six homemade bombs and two million propaganda leaflets on London in reprisal for the treatment of the *Exodus.*

Three Stern Group members were arrested at a private airport in Toussus-le-Noble near Versailles as they prepared to leave for London: Baruch Korff, thirty-three, a Russian-born New York rabbi; Judith Rosenberg, his twenty-three-year-old Hungarian secretary; and Reginald Gilbert, a onetime U.S. Army pilot from Alabama. (Gilbert was released within a few days; he was said to have provided police with information). Charges were dropped two months later when authorities admitted they could not locate any bombs.

The Royal Air Force was ordered to fire on all suspicious planes as if they were enemy aircraft. The *Daily Telegraph* reported that Air Force observation points in southern England were placed on alert.

With Britain facing the storm caused by tens of thousands of Jewish refugees on the one hand, and armed attacks of the Jewish underground on the other, a besieged London finally announced its willingness to relinquish its mandate over Palestine. At Lake Success, New York, then the home of the U.N. General Assembly, British Colonial Secretary Arthur Creech Jones warned on September 26, 1947—two weeks after the abysmal events in Hamburg—that if a solution acceptable to both the Jews and Arabs was not found, England would evacuate its entire military and civilian bureaucracy from Palestine.

The refugees on the *Exodus* can take credit for having contributed to the willingness of the British Lion to leave Eretz Yisrael.

Confrontation

The Gallows

DURING THE SUMMER of 1947, while the Haganah concentrated its efforts on illegal immigration operations, Menachem Begin, leader of the Irgun, intensified attacks on the British. The objective of his operations was to undermine the morale of British soldiers in Eretz Yisrael and disrupt the rule of law of the Mandatory government. The strategy behind Begin's revolt was to create conditions in which the British would be forced to leave the country and relinquish their Mandate. He also attained other objectives: awakening world public opinion to the situation in Palestine, arousing sympathy for the Jewish cause, and turning the Jewish problem into an issue of international proportions.

One target chosen by Begin was the thick-walled prison in Acre, among the best guarded in Palestine. In this fortress the British held approximately one-hundred prisoners of the Irgun, the Haganah, and the Stern

Identity check in Jerusalem.

Group. The British operated a gallows in the Acre fortress where Jews who had been sentenced to death by hanging were executed. The fortress in Acre was defended by police and Army units. According to the British, "the most dangerous Jewish terrorists" were imprisoned in this fortress. Acre at that time was an Arab city, well away from Jewish residential areas. There were British Army camps along the road leading to the prison, which was surrounded by broad, high walls—appropriate for a Turkish fortress built on the ruins of an ancient Crusader fort.

Units of the Irgun approached the prison in broad daylight on May 4, 1947. They were dressed in British Army uniforms and rode in a stolen British military vehicle. The British prison guards were diverted by a game of handball being played by the prisoners in the prison's main courtyard—a game intentionally organized in cooperation with their Irgun comrades outside the prison.

At that moment, the attackers exploded a barred window in the ancient walls of the prison. The 110-lb. explosive charge blew out

"Bevingrad"—the central headquarters of British administration in Jerusalem—showing barbed wire and tank traps.

the bar and prisoners began escaping through the window.

To the Irgun's dismay, a British Army unit, on its way back from a swim in the sea, happened to be passing through the area of Acre prison. They opened fire on the Irgun fighters, taking them completely by surprise. Forty-one prisoners had already escaped, while their comrades continued the battle with the British. Nine members of the Irgun were killed, among them the commander of the daring assault on Acre fortress, young Dov Cohen.

Newspapers compared the assault on the Acre prison to the fall of the Bastille. It created resounding reverberations around the world. That the Jews had liberated their prisoners from the most heavily guarded installation in British hands was a severe blow to British pride in Palestine. It also served as further proof for the U.N. of just how inflamed the situation in Palestine was.

Three of those who perpetrated the break-in were captured, sentenced to death, and hanged on July 29—at the very moment the

A search conducted by the British at the entrance to Tel Aviv on the Jerusalem–Tel Aviv road.

British troops discover a terrorist arms cache.

During the curfew in Tel Aviv.

Search carried out by the British, Jerusalem, May 1947.

Identity check and body search carried out by British troops, Jerusalem, January 1947.

refugees on the *Exodus* were making their way back to Port-de-Bouc.

The British had turned the gallows into their supreme weapon against Irgun and the Stern Group long before the break-in at the Acre prison. But not a single captured member of the more moderate Haganah or Palmach was ever hanged by them. From the British point of view, only Begin and Stern Group commander Yitzhak Shamir's men were "real Jewish terrorists." The gallows became the British Empire's most threatening weapon against the underground movement in Palestine.

Members of Irgun and the Stern Group were well aware of the fact that the hangman's noose awaited them. Nevertheless, there was no shortage of volunteers for operations. The very opposite—every hanging brought a new wave of young volunteers unintimidated by the hangman's rope.

I remember thirstily devouring every word in the newspapers about those who had been hanged. From the moment the British put

British checkpoint in Tel Aviv during the curfew (1947).

Identity check in Netanya.

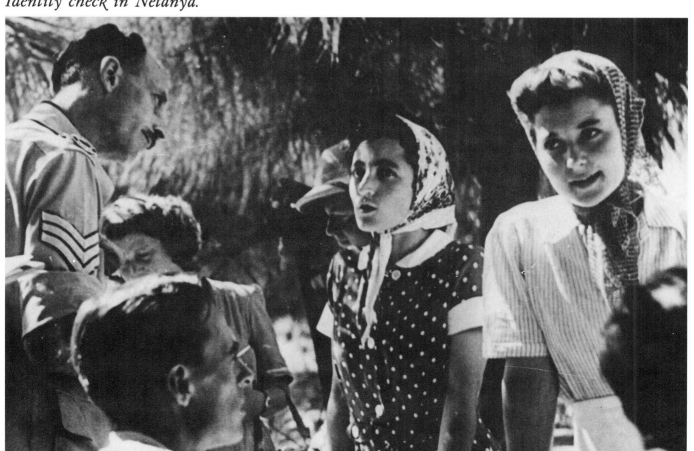

captured members of the underground on trial, the courtrooms served as a propaganda stage against the British Government. "The battle continues in the courtroom as well" was the statement made by virtually every accused. They denounced the British Government and denied its right to try them. Every defendant made this declaration at the start of the trial, then took his seat and refused to participate in the trial to its very end.

Although Ben-Gurion and Begin became sworn adversaries, the separate operations of the Haganah and Irgun complemented each other. In terms of international repercussions, the Jewish struggle in Eretz Yisrael hardly ever disappeared from the front pages of the newspapers. Just as the spirit of the refugees on the *Exodus* turned into a hurricane that shook world public opinion, so, too, the spirit of those Jews who went to the gallows in Palestine shocked the heart of the British Empire in London.

What astounded even the British was the fact that those sentenced to hang refused to appeal or request a pardon or a commuting of their sentence, even though the law allowed them to do so. The Irgun and the Stern Group fighters refused to take any step that might be construed as recognition of the British Government's right to try them. Before going to the gallows, these young fighters would sing the Jewish national anthem, "Hatikvah." One of the bravest among them, Dov Gruener, declared before his execution: "In blood and fire Judea fell. In blood and fire shall Judea arise." It was the rare fortitude of these idealistic young men that fired the imagination of other young Jews and stunned the British. In one case, two young men sentenced to death—Meir Feinstein of the Irgun and

Netanya, July 30, 1947: Nineteen days after they were kidnapped, two British sergeants were hanged by the Irgun.

Members of the Irgun being led before a British military tribunal.

bers kidnapped British officers and policemen to force the British to refrain from carrying out the sentences. However, the day after the British hanged the three who had broken into Acre, the Irgun hit back with vengeance. The Irgun hanged two British sergeants in an orange grove near Netanya, a coastal city thirty kilometers north of Tel Aviv.

This response caused a shock in London. The Manchester *Guardian* wrote: "The time has come for [the] Government to decide to leave Palestine." The British Communist newspaper, *The Daily Worker,* added: "Hangings lead to hangings . . . if it is a crime to hang British soldiers, it is also a crime to hang Jews." The pressure of British public opinion for relinquishing the Mandate over Palestine continued to mount. The British ceased using the gallows.

A senior police officer conceded at the time, "The British Army suffered greater losses in traffic accidents than in all the underground operations [in Palestine] put together. But the blows to the Empire's pride and prestige were something which could not be digested. The break-in at the Acre prison and hanging of the two sergeants were blows to our pride. The break-in at the prison gained the symbolic significance of the fall of the Bastille. And the hangings placed us, the rulers, on equal footing with the terrorists."

A straight line of unique courage links the young Jews who went to the gallows in Eretz Yisrael in that period with the hanging in Damascus some twenty years later, in entirely different circumstances, of Israeli Mosad agent Eli Cohen. All made an unusual and supreme sacrifice for an ideal—the ideal of a Jewish state.

Moshe Barazani of Lehi, the Stern Group— chose to commit suicide. On the night before they were due to be hanged in Jerusalem, they blew themselves up in their cell using a grenade that had been slipped to them inside an orange. To ensure their death, they clung to each other and allowed the grenade to explode between them.

Begin warned the British to stop the hangings of his fighters and to treat them as prisoners of war. In several instances, Irgun mem-

November 29, 1947

THE NIGHT best remembered by the Jews in Palestine was that of November 29, 1947. Throughout that entire Saturday, the Jews had closely followed the news from U.N. headquarters in Lake Success. For the previous three days, the General Assembly had been debating the proposed partition of Palestine between the Jews and the Arabs.

As midnight approached, most residents of Tel Aviv went off to sleep. Full of disappointment and disillusionment after the thirty-year British rule in Palestine, many Jews had grave doubts that their supporters would surmount the obstacles and obtain approval for partition.

Toward midnight, the radio broadcast the sensational news: the counting of votes had just been completed. Partition had been approved by the required two thirds majority. "The British mandate over Palestine will terminate as soon as possible and in any event by no later than August 1, 1948," the resolution laid down.

The news swept through Eretz Yisrael like wildfire. In Tel Aviv, people left their homes in pajamas to shout the good news: "We have a state!" Thousands thronged the streets and squares in the heart of the city. Young men and women began dancing the hora, others climbed atop buses chanting "Jewish state!" or "Free immigration!" As if by some act of magic, blue and white flags appeared from nowhere and young Jews ran through the streets, waving them jubilantly. Older people stood in groups singing the national anthem, "Hatikvah," tears of joy running down their faces. *"Mazel tov! Mazel tov!"* they congratulated each other. "The state has been born!"

That night, for the first time, the Jews of Eretz Yisrael felt that the vision of a reborn Judea, of a renewed Jewish nation like any other nation, had been realized. The Jewish community had become a sovereign state with the approval and recognition of most other nations. This feeling swept through the Jewish communities of the world, from New York to Paris. A miracle had occurred.

In Tel Aviv, cafés and stores opened in the early morning hours of November 30 to pro-

vide people who were normally used to drinking orange juice with alcoholic beverages. At the Piltz coffee house on the seashore, three thousand people drank cognac "on the house." At Hamozeg, another café known for its excellent beer, the celebrants emptied sixty barrels. Wine and beer flowed like water all over Tel Aviv. The first Jewish city had never seen so many drunk people.

The naïveté of most of the reveling Jews was so great that they believed that simply by virtue of a resolution of that eminent organization called the United Nations they already had a state. There were even those who liked to believe that the Arabs would honor the U.N. decision. At the time, there was still a great deal of respect for the United Nations. The Jews wanted to believe that an end to their suffering had come after the pogroms in Russia, the Holocaust perpetrated by the Germans, and the hangings at the hands of the British. Many saw a symbolic significance in the fact that the U.N. resolution came only a few days after the Jewish holiday of Hanukkah, which commemorates the victory of Judah Maccabee and his Hasmonean family over the Greeks.

The rude awakening from this heady drunkenness came fast. One day after the U.N. resolution, the border areas between the Jewish and Arab communities in Eretz Yisrael were in flames. On November 30, the Arabs took the initiative and attacked Jewish vehicles on the roads in the center of the country. From Jaffa, the large and powerful Arab port city, they began sniping at south Tel-Aviv. It was clear to all that the Arabs were intent on rejecting the Partition Plan and would try to prevent it by force. The seven Jews killed in

Public jubilation following the announcement of the plan for the partition of Palestine put forward by the United Nations.

123

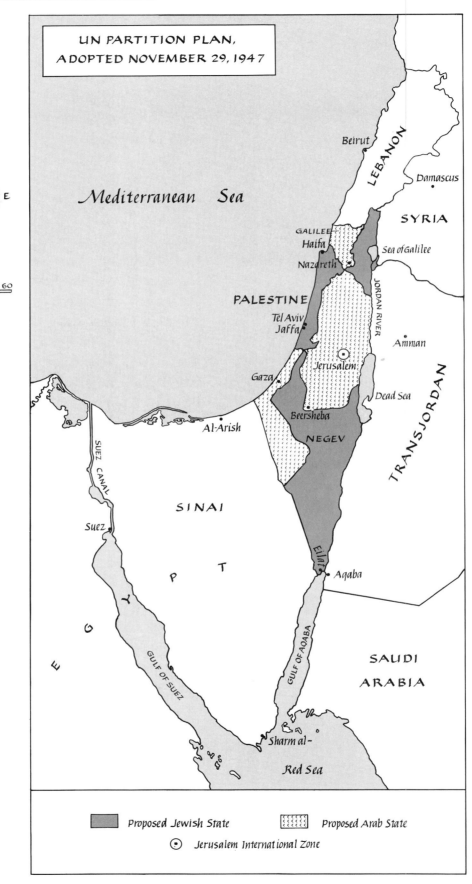

N

W — E

S

0 — MILES — 60
0 — KM — 60

Mediterranean Sea

Beirut

LEBANON

Damascus

SYRIA

GALILEE

Haifa

Sea of Galilee

Nazareth

PALESTINE

JORDAN RIVER

Tel Aviv

Jaffa

Amman

Jerusalem

Gaza

Dead Sea

Beersheba

NEGEV

TRANSJORDAN

Al-Arish

SINAI

Suez

SUEZ CANAL

E
G
Y
P
T

Eilat

Aqaba

GULF OF AQABA

GULF OF SUEZ

SAUDI

ARABIA

Sharm al-

Red Sea

Proposed Jewish State ▦ ▦ Proposed Arab State

⊙ Jerusalem International Zone

CHANGES IN ISRAEL'S FRONTIERS SINCE 1949

Mediterran

SUEZ CANAL

E
G
Y

Suez

GULF

Territory of Is.
after the 1949 ceas

Sinai-Gaza:
Twice conquered by Is
in 1956 and again in

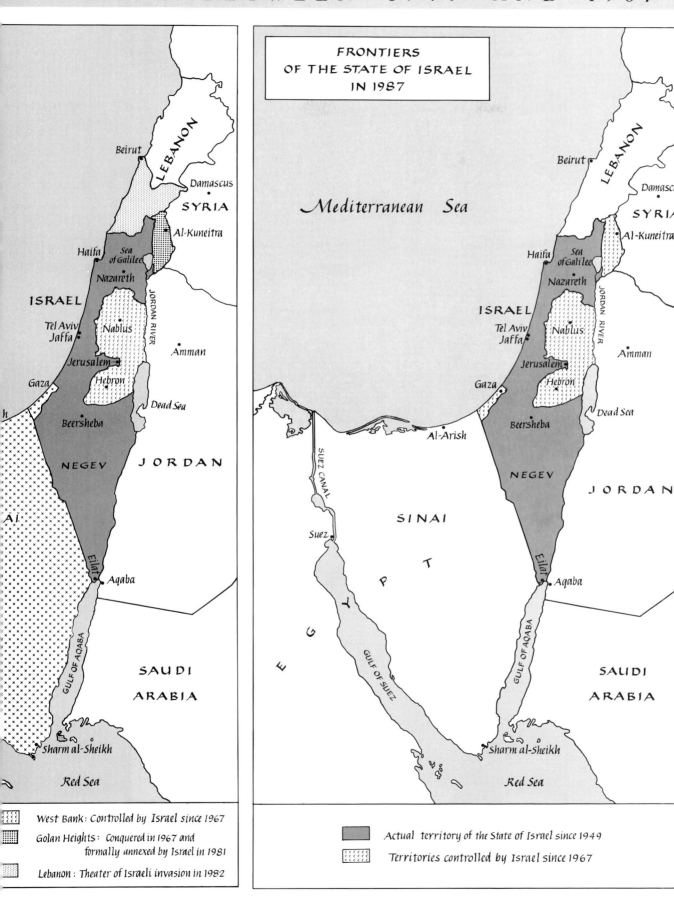

FRONTIERS
OF THE STATE OF ISRAEL
IN 1987

Mediterranean Sea

Left map labels:

Beirut
LEBANON
Damascus
SYRIA
Al-Kuneitra
Haifa
Sea of Galilee
Nazareth
ISRAEL
Tel Aviv
Jaffa
Nablus
JORDAN RIVER
Jerusalem
Amman
Gaza
Hebron
Dead Sea
Beersheba
NEGEV
JORDAN
Al
Eilat
Aqaba
GULF OF AQABA
SAUDI
ARABIA
Sharm al-Sheikh
Red Sea

Right map labels:

Beirut
LEBANON
Damascus
SYRIA
Al-Kuneitra
Haifa
Sea of Galilee
Nazareth
ISRAEL
Tel Aviv
Jaffa
Nablus
JORDAN RIVER
Jerusalem
Amman
Gaza
Hebron
Dead Sea
Beersheba
NEGEV
JORDAN
Al-Arish
SUEZ CANAL
Suez
SINAI
EGYPT
GULF OF SUEZ
GULF OF AQABA
Eilat
Aqaba
SAUDI
ARABIA
Sharm al-Sheikh
Red Sea

Legend (left):

West Bank: Controlled by Israel since 1967

Golan Heights: Conquered in 1967 and formally annexed by Israel in 1981

Lebanon: Theater of Israeli invasion in 1982

Legend (right):

Actual territory of the State of Israel since 1949

Territories controlled by Israel since 1967

December 15, 1947:
Members of the Haganah
arrested by the British in
Tel Aviv.

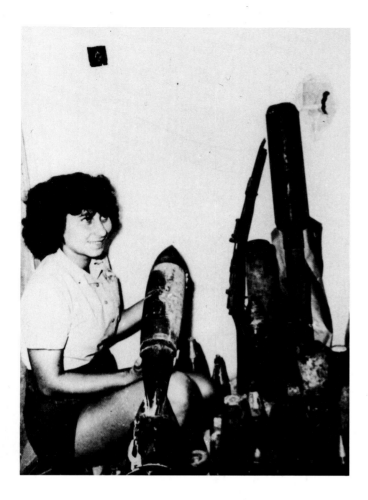

Women fighters in the kibbutzim and the Irgun.

an ambush on that Sunday were the first casualties in Israel's War of Independence. That same day, an Arab mob set fire to the Jewish business sector of Jerusalem. In Tel Aviv, our parents warned us about Arab snipers firing from Jaffa.

The War of Independence actually started that November 30. These were the first 7 of more than 6,000 Jews dead by the end of the war which finally ended with the liberation of Eilat in March 1949. The 650,000 Jews living in Eretz Yisrael at the time never dreamed they would pay the price for their independence with 1 percent of the total population. Proportionally, it was an enormous price. It was as though the present-day United States were to suffer 2,500,000 casualties all in a period of only sixteen months. A national catastrophe by any standards.

The Jews, though sensitive to human life, were nevertheless ready and willing to make any sacrifice to defend their state. The seven Jews murdered by the Arabs on Sunday, November 30, were a small part of the huge price Israel was to pay. The many thousands of deaths and injuries suffered by the Jews in the next forty years are the bitter proof of this.

Whereas the Arabs rejected the Partition Plan, Ben-Gurion and most of the Jews were willing to accept what had been given to them as if it were the greatest gift since Moses received the Ten Commandments on Mount Sinai. Ben-Gurion was willing to reach an accord with the Arabs, even though the Partition Plan stated that Jerusalem would become a "Corpus Separatum"—an entity kept separate from the Jewish and Arab states to be established in Eretz Yisrael. The boundaries of Jerusalem were to include Bethlehem in the south, Ein Karem and Moza in the west, and Shuafat in the north. The city of Jaffa was to be an Arab enclave outside the Jewish state. The way in which the population would be spread meant that the territory of the Jewish state was to include 415,000 Arab inhabitants

and an additional 90,000 Bedouins. Even so, the Jews were happy with their lot.

Ben-Gurion explained this in a speech on December 3 to the Central Committee of his party, Mapai (the workers' party), then the strongest political force in Eretz Yisrael:

"The wonder has arisen and has come into being; the nations of the world have resolved to re-establish the State of Israel. The Jewish people have always believed in this phenomenon and have waited two thousand years for it to come. This belief itself is one of the unprecedented historic wonders of the world. We know no other people that was exiled from its land and dispersed among the nations, hated, humiliated, and oppressed without respite for hundreds of years, but has nonetheless persevered in its special existence and persisted in its belief that the day would come when it would restore its independence in its own state."

In referring to the Partition, Ben-Gurion said:

"We have not been given all we wanted,

December 1947: violent clashes between Arabs and Jews in Tel Aviv.

131

Fighters of the Haganah in 1948 wearing civilian dress, equipped with small arms.

and the territory of the State of Israel has been cut back. . . . It is clear that the territory covered by the Balfour Declaration thirty years ago was four times larger. Even the territory of the "Homeland" under the 1922 Mandate was almost twice as large as that which has now been allotted to the Jewish State. Jerusalem, the heart of the Jewish people and of its history, has been placed under international domination and is surrounded on all sides by areas given to the Arab State. The mountainous areas in the Galilee have been taken from us almost in their entirety, and we have, therefore, lost not only areas of settlement, but also sources of health and stability. Over thirty [Jewish] agricultural settlements have been placed outside the area of our State, which has been given strange, weird borders. All the same, I know of no other accomplishment in the long history of our people greater than that achieved at this time. Most of the valleys of western Eretz Yisrael and most of the coastal shore have been retained by us, and these are valuable assets. A large and important portion of the sources of

133

water in the north have been restored to us and most of the barren territory in the south. The new State of Israel will extend from Dan to Eilat, about 200 kilometers [125 miles] south of Beersheba, and will lie between the two seas: the Mediterranean in the west and the Red Sea in the south. We stand before a new destiny. We will now stand as masters of our own destiny."

Ben-Gurion was even willing to reconcile himself to the internationalization of Jerusalem, but he specifically stated:

"With the establishment of international rule in Jerusalem and its environs, and the separation from the Jewish state, Jerusalem will not cease being what it has always been to the Jewish people—from the days of King David right up to the present—'the heart of the Jewish people.' It has not been made the capital of the Jewish state—but it was and will continue for all time to be the spiritual capital of the Jewish people—the center of the entire Jewish people—both that in Eretz Yisrael and that in the Diaspora. Jerusalem must be the heart and soul of the Jews of the world."

In short, Ben-Gurion was willing to make do with the bare minimum granted the Jews in Eretz Yisrael by the U.N. He was even willing to forego control of Jerusalem, the important thing being that Jews would gain a country of their own, small as it might be. He explained this in the same speech:

"The borders of the State under Jewish rule —beginning with the days of the Judges and extending all the way to Bar Kochba— changed unceasingly, and there are few terms that are less clear than the term "historic" borders. From the early days, the borders of Jewish independence would retreat and advance in accordance with constant political changes and even the degree of independence was not always permanent. . . ."

Ben-Gurion hoped, and his supporters hoped even more, that this minimum which the United Nations had decreed as the territory of the State of Israel would, in the end, be the basis for an agreement with its Arab neighbors and peace treaties with the adjacent Arab states. Sadly, this hope was not to be realized.

But Ben-Gurion's observation that the borders of the Jewish state "changed unceasingly" indeed proved to be true in the following years. He himself determined later on, despite the opposition of the superpowers, that Jerusalem would be under Israeli rule. In 1967, Ben-Gurion had the good fortune to see Israel liberate the Old City of Jerusalem, conquered by the Arab Legion in 1948. Ever since the Six-Day War in 1967, Israel has also controlled Judea and Samaria and the Golan Heights, and no one knows whether these will be Israel's final borders—or whether she will have to withdraw from these territories. The State of Israel twice held the Sinai Desert up to the Suez Canal: once in 1956, as a result of the Suez Campaign, and a second time from 1967 to 1982, when Sinai was returned to Egypt in exchange for a peace agreement.

It is doubtful whether there is another example in modern history of a state whose territorial borders have changed as many times, in so brief a period, as have the State of Israel's. It is possible that this is the outcome of a very unusual historic case—the case of a people who returned to their land after many hundreds of years, only to find that other occupants had laid claim to the same territory.

But the Arabs made a fatal error; they decided that the Jews were entitled to nothing at all. This was a resolve they would seek to ensure by force of arms and terror. On December 11, eleven Jews were murdered and, on the fourteenth, fourteen more were killed. Thousands of Jews left their destroyed homes in the suburbs of Tel Aviv, Jerusalem, and Haifa. The British Army did not intervene to prevent the Arabs from perpetrating their acts of terror. On the contrary, the British encouraged the chaos which reigned, presumably with the intention of sabotaging the Partition. In any event, it appeared they wished to secure Arab superiority. The flames spread throughout Eretz Yisrael. Since the British still ruled the country, Ben-Gurion secretly ordered that everyone possible enlist in the ranks of the Haganah. By the end of December, the total number conscripted by the Haganah reached 7,500.

Ben-Gurion issued a decree: "Not a single Jewish position or settlement is to be evacuated. We shall hold them to the last man!"

The Purchase of Weapons

AS THE JEWS prepared for the War of Independence, procuring desperately needed weapons was at the top of their list of priorities. But they were plagued by two difficulties: the British secret service and a severe lack of funds.

These days, with rumors that Israel possesses nuclear weapons built in its French-supplied reactor at Dimona and a sophisticated weapons production system that has manufactured the Uzi submachine gun and Merkava tank, it is almost impossible to believe how limited the weapons of the Yishuv were in 1948. The Haganah boasted with pride of its crude copy of a British Sten submachine gun.

In the United States, the Haganah acquired old weapons-manufacturing machines from scrap yards and smuggled them under the eyes of British Customs as industrial machines. British weapons were taken from arsenals; at the end of World War II, the Haganah had ordered all its volunteers to steal as many weapons as possible for transporting to Palestine.

Directing this operation, as he had so suc-cessfully done with Mosad Aliyah Bet, was Shaul Avigur.

Convoys loaded with weapons from British military depots in Belgium, Italy, and Germany deposited their precious cargo in meticulously prepared hideouts in Marseilles, Toulouse, and Pau. One such arsenal was accidentally uncovered by French police at a farm in Villeneuve-sur-Lot and confiscated. Local Haganah officials hurried to French authorities; as with the *Exodus,* the French again turned a blind eye and agreed to return the weapons, provided that the Haganah immediately left France. A Haganah convoy took the weapons to Italy, where they were stored on the outskirts of Milan in an arms depot acquired from the British.

In 1947 Ben-Gurion sent to Italy a young blond-haired man named Munia Mardor; possessing the sober elegant bearing of a prosperous lawyer, he had been instructed to secretly ship the weapons to Palestine.

Mardor set up secret workshops at which volunteers packed the arms—machine guns, submachine guns, dynamite—into cases that

Tel Aviv, March 1948: the manufacture of the first homemade Israeli armored cars.

Homemade flamethrowers manufactured by the Irgun in 1947.

were loaded into heavy equipment cases used to transport steamrollers, and then shipped to Haifa as civilian machinery. Neither the Arab dockworkers in Haifa nor the British inspectors ever discovered the true nature of the cargo.

In this way, Mardor was able through the end of 1947 to ship the Yishuv 200 Bren machine guns with spare parts, 1,000 British rifles, 500 German rifles, 400 submachine guns, 500 rifles, and 1.5 million rounds of ammunition. In early 1948, another 555 tons of weapons, ammunitions, and explosives were sent to Palestine from Italy.

Avigur and Mardor believed, correctly, that the fate of their still unborn state lay in their hands. That belief was reinforced in a handwritten note from Ben-Gurion to Mardor on September 30, 1947: "To all comrades in Europe, I ask that you give the bearer of this message all the help he may require to fulfill his mission, which at this very moment and in the context of the situation in which we find ourselves is of the highest importance to our continued existence."

The situation changed dramatically after November 29, 1947. The surprise support of the Soviet Union for Partition and a Jewish state gave the Jews access to Czechoslovakian arms sources seeking to destabilize the British presence in the Middle East. With a go-ahead from Moscow, Prague began to sell weapons to both Jews and Arabs—with the Jews paying elevated prices.

The first Yishuv arms-buying mission to Prague in the spring of 1948 included a decisive young man with sparkling blue eyes named Ehud Avriel, a native Czech and a born diplomat.

On the eve of his trip, Avriel told Ben-Gurion that the Czechs, knowing the Yishuv's desperate financial condition, were demanding a million dollars in advance. After a few worried moments of consideration, Ben-Gurion told him, "Give them a deferred check. If

Members of the Haganah in training.

we win the war, we'll have the means to honor it. And if we lose . . ." His voice trailed off.

Using that check, Avriel purchased six million dollars of arms in Prague—and the debts were all honored. Because pre-statehood Israel faced an international arms embargo, the weapons were officially listed as heading for Ethiopia; they reached Israel via a circuitous route through Hungary and Yugoslavia.

May 1948: homemade mortar built by the Haganah.

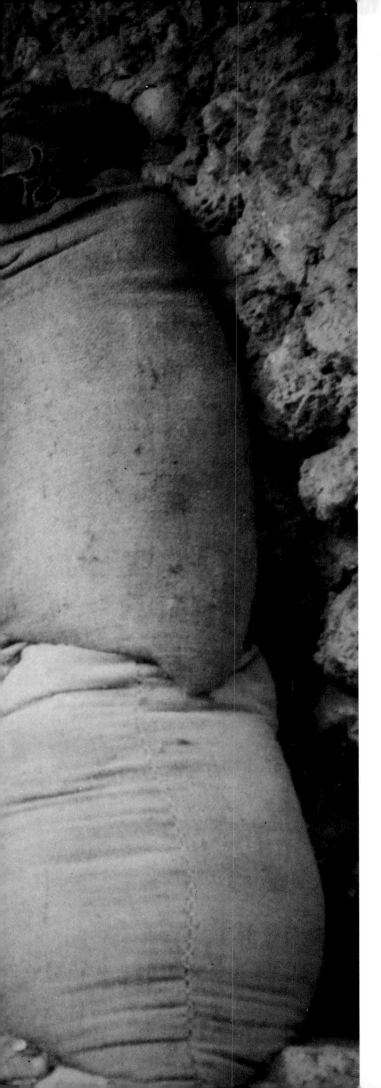

Israeli Setbacks in Jerusalem

THE REVERSES Israel suffered in the defense of Jerusalem were extremely distressing. Nowhere did the close cooperation between the British and the Arabs stand out more than in the city the Jews regard as the heart of their nation. On February 1, 1948, British policemen were involved in the explosion of a truck full of dynamite at the building housing *The Palestine Post,* Jerusalem's English-language Jewish daily paper.

Three weeks later, at six in the morning, a small British Army convoy was seen moving through the center of Jewish Jerusalem along King George V Street. Two armored cars stopped at Ben Yehuda Street while the rest of the convoy made off. A few moments later, a deafening explosion was heard throughout Jerusalem. The trucks contained a huge amount of explosives, and their detonation destroyed

Jerusalem, December 1947: Even Orthodox Jews took up arms in defense of their capital.

141

Street fighting in Jerusalem in 1948.

half a block. The dimension of the killings was ghastly: more than 50 innocent civilians were slain and over 120 wounded.

From all the evidence collected, it was clear that this act of terrorism was British-made or perpetrated by the Arabs under British guidance. The effect on morale was severe; David Ben-Gurion, who came to Jerusalem from Tel Aviv in one of the convoys that same day, wrote in his diary: "The first thing I did was to go to Ben Yehuda Street. [There was] destruction such as I had never imagined, I couldn't recognize the streets. It was horrendous and awful. . . ."

On the second day of March, the Haganah went out on a reprisal raid against the Arabs in Jerusalem. A Haganah unit tried to strike at Arab traffic on the Ramallah–Latrun Road. Nineteen people went out to set an ambush

Jerusalem, 1948: women in the Medical Corps of the Army.

142

An explosion in the Jewish Quarter of Jerusalem in 1948.

for Arab vehicles, only to find they had been ambushed themselves. All but three of the Jews were killed; their bodies were brought to Hadassah Hospital on Mount Scopus under British police escort. It was almost impossible to identify them; they had been deliberately and cruelly mutilated. It was a gruesome sight, one that clearly reminded the Jews of the extent of Arab hatred toward them. It was a sight the Jews would know time and again in future encounters in Palestine.

About a week later, the Arabs struck once more in the heart of Jerusalem. This time it was in the grounds of the Jewish Agency building; thirteen people met their death and another hundred were injured. An Arab driver working for the American Consulate had managed to get a car bomb into the guarded compound.

A tragedy of even greater proportions occurred in Jerusalem on the way to Mount Scopus, which was isolated and cut off from the New City. Access to it—including Hebrew University and Hadassah Hospital, which for years had served both Jews and Arabs—required passing through hostile Arab territory. As clashes escalated, the Haganah maintained contact with these institu-

Snipers claim another victim in Jerusalem.

tions, using convoys of buses and ambulances, escorted by armored cars, to reach them.

On April 14 the British—who had promised to secure the convoys—reported to the Haganah that the road was clear; the next group could make its way to Mount Scopus. But as the convoy entered the Arab neighborhood of Sheikh Jarrah, an attack broke out. For hours Arabs threw hand grenades and Molotov cocktails into the convoy and shot at the wounded trying to escape. British soldiers standing by not only failed to stop the Arabs from continuing their assault, but actually blocked the Haganah forces trying to save the doomed convoy. Before the unmoved eyes of British soldiers and officers, the Arabs set fire to the vehicles of the convoy and murdered every man and woman who tried to escape from the flames.

Of the 105 people in the convoys, 77 were slain—doctors, nurses, and teachers.

Nearly two decades would pass before Israel regained control of Mount Scopus. The massacre of the "Hadassah Convoy" was a shattering horror for the hundred thousand Jews of Jerusalem and demoralizing for the rest of Jewish Palestine. But the murder in cold blood of doctors and nurses made it clear to the Jews what they could expect from the Arabs unless they won the struggle. I remember the sad, anxious faces of people in Tel Aviv.

Yet the next Arab blow was even greater. On May 12 King Abdullah's Arab Legion opened a decisive offensive on Gush Etzion, a group of four kibbutzim defending Jerusalem's southern flank that had been under siege since December 1947. Ben-Gurion was insistent that Gush Etzion, already cut off and isolated, not be evacuated. Holding down Arab forces in that area, he figured, would

The last of the fighting for the control of Jerusalem (1948).

146

147

prevent them from attacking Jerusalem. In January 1948, the Haganah sent a reinforcement of thirty-five men on foot through the hills to the Gush. An Arab shepherd spotted them and spread the alarm, which brought out hundreds of Arab villagers. They encircled the group and eventually murdered all thirty-five of them, brutally mutilating their bodies.

Despite all this, the kibbutzim held firm and for many months controlled the Hebron–Jerusalem Road, even though supplies could only be brought in by air.

Just three days before the British were to leave Palestine, King Abdullah's Arab Legion vehicles, with the aid of hundreds of Arabs from Hebron and the surrounding villages, launched a violent assault on the settlements. They called for help: "The situation is dreadful. We're going crazy here. We are fighting a Massada-like battle. . . ."

But Ben-Gurion and the Haganah were unable to assist. Ben-Gurion was able only to send them the following message: "We all look in awe and admiration on the unequal struggle you are fighting. Your earlier battles not only brought great respect, but also helped directly and indirectly to save Jerusalem. We feel sure that you will continue your brave struggle and defense without flinching."

On the morning of May 14, the British High Commissioner left Jerusalem for the last time, in an armor-plated Daimler. That morning Gush Etzion fell, after 250 of its defenders had been killed. Some of the women on the kibbutzim committed suicide, using hand grenades; they did not want to fall into the hands of the Arab mob whose chants of "Etbach-al-Yahud"—"Massacre the Jews"—rang in their ears.

On trucks, donkeys, and camels the Arabs dragged off the cabinets, furniture, doors, and windows they had torn out from the ruined houses on the kibbutzim. The legion took 184 men prisoner to Hebron on the way to Jordan.

This blow failed to deter Ben-Gurion from going to the Tel Aviv Museum that same afternoon and reading the Declaration of Independence of the State of Israel. But he recorded in his diary: "At four P.M. Jewish independence was declared and the state established. Its fate lies in the hands of the defense forces. Around the country there was great joy and happiness, and once again I was a mourner among the jubilant as I had been on November 29."

An even greater setback was yet to come—the fall of the Jewish Quarter and the entire Old City of Jerusalem to the Arab Legion.

The Arab Flight

EVEN BEFORE the proclamation of the State of Israel, hundreds of thousands of Arabs abandoned their homes, fields, shops, and orchards and fled. Between January and May of 1948, the problem that has since weighed like a dark cloud over the whole of the Middle East —that of the Arab refugees—was created, a problem that still remains to be solved.

To this day the experts have difficulty in explaining this flight. For the Arabs fled not only from towns and villages in areas allotted the Jewish state, but also from territory allocated by the U.N. to the Palestinian Arab state.

Leaders of the Arab population in Palestine had no doubts that they could defeat the Jews. Thus invasion of the regular Arab armies on May 15 was preceded by a lengthy period of sporadic individual incursions by Arab bands across the borders, vowing "to throw out the Jews and annihilate them."

On January 9, 1948, an Arab force of several hundred invaded Galilee from Syria. Their aim was to capture at least one Jewish settlement, preferably Kibbutz Kfar Szold. The Lebanese Defense Minister himself closely observed this offensive.

On the twentieth of the same month, 500 heavily armed Syrians attacked Yehiam in western Galilee.

Four days later the Palestine Liberation Army invaded with a force of 750 men, arriving on machine-gun trucks on the outskirts of Nablus. The British declared that they were no longer in control of the situation. Three weeks later this force attacked Tirat Zevi in the Beit Shean valley.

On February 25, Fawzi al-Kaukji, commander of the Arab Redemption Army, invaded Eretz Yisrael with one thousand men equipped with cannon, and set up his headquarters in Nablus. Over two hundred British Army deserters stationed in Palestine joined these Arab groups.

The invading forces boosted the morale of the local Arabs, leading them to believe that the day of victory was at hand. The British did nothing to prevent the incursion, which had been armed and backed by Jordan, Iraq, Syria,

and Lebanon. Yet these attacks usually ended in failure, though the Jews suffered scores of casualties almost daily. The Arabs thus proved from the start that they would do everything they could to destroy the Jewish community in Eretz Yisrael even before it had the opportunity of declaring its statehood.

Arab leaders instilled in their Palestinian brethren the belief that the Arab invasion would be a two-week pleasure trip. In Arab headquarters, it was said that King Abdullah's Legion could get to Tel Aviv within one week and that Haifa could be taken within two. Senior British officers hoped and believed this would be the case. In keeping with the best tradition of Middle Eastern imagination, stories were spread of how Egypt's King Farouk was preparing a white horse on which to ride for his victorious entrance to Tel Aviv, where "the Arabs would take blond Jewish girls clad in shorts for themselves."

I remember these rumors of the "Arab plans" in Tel Aviv, some of them even appearing in the Hebrew press. To some extent, they help explain the flight of the Arabs: convinced that they would soon be returning, they had no doubt they were leaving homes for a few days, perhaps a few weeks, at most a few months. They believed that within a short time they would come back together with the victorious Arab armies, not only to their own homes, but to plunder and take Jewish homes for themselves.

The Arab leadership explicity encouraged this hope. In each case where the Arabs faced Jewish counterattacks, principally by the Haganah and also by Irgun and the Stern Group, Arab leaders advised the inhabitants to flee, because "you will soon return and avenge yourselves."

In contrast with regular acts of cruelty per-

A British Army deserter amid Arab fighters.

petrated by the Arabs, there was only one instance in which Jews were accused of a massacre of civilians. On April 9 Irgun and Lehi units attacked the village of Deir Yassin, which lies west of Jerusalem, and killed 240 Arabs, half of them women. The Haganah immediately condemned the act as a "massacre." This event is still the subject of heated and bitter debates among Israelis to this day.

There are those who attribute the Arab flight to stories of the atrocities which were bandied about by the Arabs in greatly exaggerated form following Deir Yassin. However, it is hard to believe that Arab residents of Haifa and Jaffa left these big cities only because of the story of one village.

These two key cities, the most important in Eretz Yisrael after Jerusalem, fell into Jewish hands only a few days apart, during the last days of April 1948. Haifa was the most important port in Palestine and one of the most important in the entire eastern Mediterranean basin. The Arabs controlled the port and the trade that passed through it, although the British held the port until their final evacuation of Palestine. On April 21, however, the

Moshe Dayan perched on his command jeep in the spring of 1948.

British announced that they were leaving their positions in the city itself. The Haganah, prepared for this, began shelling Arab positions and stormed key positions in the city. This was the first true test of power between the Jews and Arabs: to determine who would control the strategic seaport.

Within twenty-four hours, tens of thousands of Haifa's Arabs began fleeing their homes in the downtown area, traveling by car, on foot, and by sea. They left for nearby Acre and distant Beirut—the same Beirut that would later become the capital of Yasser Arafat's PLO until he was expelled by the Israelis on August 21, 1982, with ten thousand terrorists.

The Arab community of Palestine was severely jolted by the fall of Haifa. Three days after it fell, the Irgun, which was already operating in the open although the British Army still controlled Jaffa and Tel Aviv, mounted an attack on Jaffa. Until then, the Arabs had threatened Tel Aviv incessantly for several months. Not a day went by without firing and shelling in the southern suburbs of the largest Jewish city. I remember my father, as a member of the Haganah, taking his post in one of the positions defending the front line between Jaffa and Tel Aviv. The whine of bullets in flight in the streets of south Tel Aviv and the little pings when they hit the walls of our home still ring in my ear.

The British tried to save Jaffa by opening fire on the Jews. But the battle was decided by the fact that tens of thousands of Arabs fled from Jaffa. They abandoned the city in which they and their forefathers had lived for hundreds of years; Jaffa is one of the oldest cities in the world, from the shores of which the biblical prophet Jonah left on the journey in which he was said to be swallowed by a whale. The Arabs boarded boats and ships and made off for Lebanon and the Gaza Strip.

The largest Arab city in Eretz Yisrael officially signed a deed of surrender on May 13, six and a half months after it had opened hostilities on Tel Aviv. Together with other children, I hurried to Jaffa a few days later. We were shocked by the signs of destruction everywhere. The beautiful city, with its tree-lined boulevards, its houses with their massive heavy doors and arched windows, was almost totally deserted, a ghost town. Only a few thousand Arabs remained in Jaffa. Under the Partition Plan, the city was to remain an independent Arab enclave within the Jewish state. Now the Arabs had lost Jaffa completely.

The Arab flight disturbed and bothered Ben-Gurion. Not that he was sorry—but he wanted to know what had caused them to flee from Jaffa and Haifa. On May 1 he went on an inspection of Haifa and learned from the local Haganah commanders that of the thirty-five thousand Arabs in Haifa on the eve of the Jewish offensive, only about ten thousand remained. "They continue to flee," Ben-Gurion was told, leaving behind huge stores of food that the Haganah immediately took control of.

"Toward evening," Ben-Gurion wrote in his diary, "I went through the Arab neighborhoods once again. It was a shocking but fantastic sight. A dead city, an urban corpse. Only in one place did we see two old people sitting in a half-empty store. . . . there was not a soul around, apart from a few stray cats. . . . Why did tens of thousands of people leave their city, their homes, and their worldly possessions in such panic, without sufficient cause? What caused this flight? Could it have been simply an order from above? It does not seem possible that the immensely rich—and some of the richest people in the country lived here—would abandon all their material assets just because somebody gave them an order. Was it really fear?"

Soldiers of the Arab Redemption Army led by al-Kaukji: May 1948.

153

Some 800,000 Arabs took to the roads in 1948 to flee their homes in Palestine.

1947: the call for a Holy War.

Arab guerrilla armed with grenades.

Ben-Gurion's questions prove that the issue perplexed him. But no answer is forthcoming. There is room to assume that the Arabs of Eretz Yisrael believed the promises made by their leaders that victory over the Jews was certain. Never in their worst nightmares did they consider the possibility that they would not return as victors.

On June 5 Ben-Gurion received a report on the magnitude of the Arab flight. The numbers were astounding. A total of 123,000 Arabs had deserted 155 villages within the original territory of the State; 22,000 Arabs left 35 villages outside the State of Israel.

In the five cities within the territory of the state—Haifa, Beit Shean, Tiberias, Safed, and Tzemach—77,000 fled. Another 73,000 left Jaffa and Acre, two cities that were to have remained outside the Jewish state. And 40,000 Arabs fled Jerusalem. In all, 335,000 Arabs left their homes, 200,000 from the territory which the United Nations had assigned to the Jewish state. At the end of the war the total number of Arab refugees amounted to approximately 800,000.

There were many who advised Ben-Gurion to discuss the matter with the Arab states to arrange for resettlement of the refugees in those states. This idea has been raised repeatedly over the last forty years, but the Arab governments never seemed to want to resolve the problem. And many of the thousands of Jewish refugees who left Arab states in the years that followed were resettled in the abandoned Arab homes of Jaffa, Haifa, Acre, and other towns. One and a half months after the conquest of Jaffa, Ben-Gurion clearly stated his opinion in a cabinet meeting: "I believe that their [the Arabs'] return must be prevented. We must settle Jaffa. Jaffa will become a Jewish city. War is war. We didn't want the war. Tel Aviv didn't make war on Jaffa. Jaffa made war on Tel Aviv. . . . Those who declared war on us must take full responsibility for their folly and their failure. . . ."

Only in isolated cases did the Haganah encourage Arabs to leave their villages and towns, and only after the example set by the Arabs of Jaffa and Haifa.

Ben-Gurion spoke openly to his fellow leaders on Tuesday, May 11, 1948: "The Arab islands in the Jewish expanses must be destroyed—for example, the cities of Ramle and Lod." Ben-Gurion feared that with the impending Arab invasion, these towns would tie down Jewish forces and become a source of "special danger." Ben-Gurion raised this idea in the course of preparation for the decisive battle for Jerusalem. "The struggle for Jerusalem is the struggle for Eretz Yisrael, not only because of its historic importance, but also for strategic reasons. . . . it is not enough to have a road between Tel Aviv and Jerusalem. . . . territorial continuity is necessary. . . . this war has already proved that a Jewish Jerusalem is not viable without an unbroken link with the Jewish state."

The Israeli offensive began on July 11, and ensured "territorial continuity" between Tel Aviv and Jerusalem. That day Ben-Gurion returned to his headquarters after a three-day illness. The months of strain had taken their toll of him, and there were those who said he was depressed as well as fatigued.

The Israeli objective was the conquest of Lod and Ramle, two Arab towns defended by the "Arab Legion" that controlled the road between Tel Aviv and Jerusalem. Palmach General Yigal Allon commanded the operation, but the actual breakthrough was made by a young battalion commander, Lieutenant Colonel Moshe Dayan. He led commando Battalion 89, which broke through and then stormed Lod.

Dayan and Allon, the outstanding officers of the War of Independence, fought together as commanders side by side. Lod and Ramle fell in two days. "These are great deeds," Ben-Gurion wrote with awe. "Almost unbelievable . . ."

On July 15 Moshe Dayan was called in to give a personal report to Ben-Gurion on the successful action. He told the Prime Minister that the battalion had 400 men, of whom 250

July 11, 1948: Surrender of the Arab town of Ramle, on the way from Tel Aviv to Jerusalem.

were fighters. Dayan described to Ben-Gurion how he had entered the Arab city of Lod with 150 combatants equipped with eight jeeps, six half-tracks (trucks with wheels enclosed within a rotating track), and one cannon-mounted armored car he had taken earlier as booty from the Arab Legion. The soldiers painted the words "the Terrible Tiger" on the armored car. Dayan himself commanded the attack from one of the jeeps.

The amazing part of Dayan's offensive was that he had driven his battalion into the town of Lod, his men firing in all directions without any preparation—the style of commando operation that became Dayan's trademark for many years. The ease with which Lod fell, despite its being defended by soldiers of the Arab Legion, surprised everyone. Thus Ben-Gurion wanted to hear about the action from Dayan himself.

Up to then their acquaintance had been superficial—from that moment, it was fateful. Ben-Gurion told Dayan he had carried out a "guerrilla-type operation" and that this was

157

not the way to conduct an operation. "The triumph was purely fortuitous," he reprimanded Dayan.

But Dayan replied, "With the Arabs, this is the way one must and can go on the offensive, to achieve a quick breakthrough, to throw them off balance." Ben-Gurion was favorably impressed. He appointed Dayan commander of the Jerusalem Region a short time later, to replace David Shaltiel. Subsequently, Ben-Gurion sent Dayan as his representative to secret negotiations with King Abdullah.

Dayan's forces also took control of Eretz Yisrael's main international airport, Lod. "Who knows whether the Government of Israel could have built an airport such as this in ten years!" Ben-Gurion said in amazement. After his death in 1973, the name of what is still Israel's principal international airport was changed to Ben-Gurion.

Allon and Dayan's units also captured the important police station between Ramle and Lod, which became Israel's central prison. It would be the place in which Israel would carry out the only execution in its history; the Nazi criminal, Adolf Eichmann, was hanged there in the summer of 1962, after having been captured in Argentina and put on trial in Jerusalem.

Once again, in Lod and Ramle, the majority of the Arab inhabitants fled. This time, however, the Israelis encouraged their flight. Israel wanted this area, halfway to Jerusalem, under complete Jewish domination.

Thirty thousand Arab refugees followed in the footsteps of the retreating Jordanian Arab Legion. They would join the hundreds of thousands of other Arab refugees who paid the price for accepting the promises of Arab leaders of a "quick victory over Tel Aviv."

Ben-Gurion issued strict orders regarding Arab property. He still hoped it would be possible to make another attempt to recapture the Old City. Moshe Dayan was the man for the task, Ben-Gurion said. He had his eye on this young officer and in 1953 would appoint him as chief of staff. In the north, the Israeli Army was about to conquer Nazareth. Ben-Gurion's order to the commanders was unequivocal: "You must establish a special force that will deal mercilessly and if necessary use machine guns against any Jew, and especially against any Jewish soldier, who tries to loot or desecrate any Christian or Moslem holy place." Israeli soldiers later took Nazareth, and since then, Israel has safeguarded the sites that are so holy to Christianity.

The Intelligence

SPECIAL EMPHASIS was placed in the Haganah on the "Shai," a Hebrew acronym for the words "Information Agency." Gathering intelligence information on both the British and the Arabs was vital for this underground organization, just as it was for the Irgun, which established its own intelligence agency. As the war with the Arabs approached, the need to gather information on their armies and military plans became even more vital. Volunteers willing to go on secret missions among the Arabs were drawn from the ranks of the Palmach. They were young Jews who had been born in, or whose parents had come from the Arab states and who had immigrated to Eretz Yisrael. They were dark like the Arabs and spoke fluent Arabic.

From 1942 on, the Palmach established a secret unit comprised of future spies, whose code name was "Hashachar" (the sunrise). Yitzhak Sadeh and Yigal Allon personally recruited these agents. Their first commander was an extremely competent officer, Yeroham Cohen. Their job was not only to spy, but to be ready at all times to infiltrate the enemy's rear dressed as Arabs, and to carry out acts of sabotage. When the Intelligence Branch of the Israeli Army was later established, this group was attached to it as a special unit under the code name "I.S.18." It became an important unit in the Israelis' intelligence community, producing such men as Eli Cohen, who was hanged in 1965 for his remarkable spy mission in Damascus. Syrian counterintelligence discovered that Cohen had penetrated the country's leadership under the guise of a rich, politically ambitious businessman. But Eli Cohen was not the first Israeli spy hanged by the Arabs.

The "Arab Department" was the name given to the Palmach's espionage and sabotage unit, one which trained its members in the different Arabic dialects and customs that vary from country to country. They dressed and behaved like Arabs. "Each of these secret agents is worth an entire battalion," the senior commanders of the Palmach would say. On May 7, 1948, Ben-Gurion wrote in his diary that there were thirty-seven agents of this

Israeli agents disguised as Arabs.

kind of which "nineteen are ripe" (ready for operations).

From the start however, operating Jewish agents on the Arab side met with failure which cost several lives.

Jerusalem-born David Mizrachi took the Arab name Daoud. Ezra Horin, known in Arabic as Izat, was born in Asmara, the capital of Eritrea. They were both a little over twenty. In May 1948 they were sent to the

Gaza Strip a few days after the Egyptian Army had invaded it and began advancing on Ashkelon and Ashdod on their way to Tel Aviv. It was important to know everything possible about the Egyptian Army and, if possible, conduct sabotage operations against it. They were to return to Israel within a week.

But both were captured by the Egyptian Army and shot to death at the entrance to the city of Gaza on August 22, 1948. Their commanders learned of their death through the Egyptian press, which reported that "Ezra Horin of Tel Aviv admitted that he brought a canteen full of typhus and dysentery germs with him to Gaza, intending to dump it into a well and poison the whole Egyptian Army."

Yet there were also some important successes. Agents of Hashachar managed to penetrate Arab capitals from Beirut to Damascus, Amman to Cairo. Yaakov Nimrodi, one of the commanders of the unit, later told me: "Hashachar conducted intelligence operations in Arab states the details of which cannot even now, forty years later, be published. Each of the intelligence corps the State of Israel has today—the Mosad, the Shin Bet, and Military Intelligence—had its roots in this unit.

One of the most successful agents, code-named "Yaakuba," divided his time between Beirut and Damascus dressed in Arab garb, sending back important reports and information to Israel. Years later, he said in the book *The Arabists of the Palmach,* "In Damascus and Beirut it was the practice to hang those who had been sentenced to death in the yards outside the courts or in city squares. This was usually true of criminal offenders. Their bodies would hang all day, particularly if they were ruthless criminals or 'spies,' to serve as a deterrent to others. Throughout the time I spent in Beirut and Damascus, I lived with the thought that one of these days I might be caught and suffer a similar fate. It is difficult for me to explain why I felt impelled from time to time, some times quite frequently, to

Members of the Israeli Intelligence Service disguised as Arabs.

get close up and watch these morbid executions. I would stand staring at the victim's body as though transfixed. The thought that I might myself one day be put to death in the city square in the same way preoccupied me a great deal for days on end. I spent a lot of time contemplating what my own reactions would be."

Yaakuba returned to Israel after completing the full length of his assignment in Beirut and Damascus.

Fighters on the road to Jerusalem during the battle for the hills of Castel in the spring of 1948.

The Battle
for the Road
to Jerusalem

ANYONE DRIVING to Jerusalem today sees strange rusting wrecks along the road called Shaar Hagai (Bab el Wad in Arabic). These are the remnants of the Jewish armored vehicles burned by the Arabs in the course of the Israeli attempt to break through to Jerusalem during the siege of 1948. The battle for the road to Jerusalem started almost immediately after the U.N. resolution of November 29, 1947. The forty-mile stretch separating Tel Aviv and Jerusalem was dotted with a large number of Arab towns, such as Lod and Ramle. Hostile Arab villages sat atop the hills on the winding road. Castel, a high point on which an ancient Roman fortress once stood, and which controlled access to Jerusalem, was in Arab hands.

Supplies for Jerusalem had to be transported via this route to provide the bare necessities for the 100,000 Jews living there (as against 34,000 Moslems and 13,000 Christians). The British absolved themselves of any responsibility for Jewish vehicles driving between Jerusalem and Tel Aviv; so armed Arab gangs fired indiscriminately on the traffic, ambushing Jewish trucks and buses and inflicting casualties. Yet Haganah men escorting these vehicles were forced to hide their weapons or see them confiscated by the British. One convoy didn't reach Jerusalem until ten days after starting out from Tel Aviv.

Ben-Gurion gave orders that, come what might, convoys to Jerusalem be protected and, above all, that a supply of food sufficient for a prolonged siege be prepared. At the time Jerusalem only had food supplies for two weeks.

A convoy of one hundred trucks was assembled. The big question was whether to include three tons of cigarettes. After much debate, the Israelis, who are among the heaviest smokers in the world, decided that cigarettes were an essential. A time would eventually come in the course of the long siege when smokers searched for cigarette butts in garbage cans.

Jerusalem required 4,500 tons of bare supplies each month. Water, bread, and gasoline had to be rationed. From February 1948 Jerusalem had no meat, fish, eggs, or milk, except that intended for children. Jerusalem's water supply and pumping stations were in Arab hands. So the Jewish residents were instructed to clean out the water holes that had been dug in their backyards years earlier to collect rainwater—back when Jerusalem had no properly regulated municipal water supply. The Jewish commanders calculated that if water could be collected in all the water holes, it could provide each resident with ten quarts of water per day for 115 days. These precautions were well-founded; as soon as the British evacuated on May 15, the Arabs disconnected the water supply to Jerusalem.

It was also decided to cut back on the use of electricity in Jerusalem because of the shortage of gasoline. Restaurants and homes were heated with wood; bus service was re-

164

On May 15, 1948, the Arabs cut off Jerusalem's water supply.

duced and the use of private cars prohibited. Jerusalemites became accustomed to walking. Kerosene was rationed for private use.

The city gradually became a ghost town. Jerusalem, once the lively British capital in Palestine, an international meeting place for the whole Mideast and a major tourist attraction, became a shadow of its former self.

Jerusalemites, who had long grown accustomed to the firing of Arab machine guns and mortars, now tasted actual cannon fire for the first time in the city's history, on the Sabbath eve of April 9, 1948. An Iraqi officer fired four French 75-mm cannons into the heart of the New City from a nearby mountain top. These cannons, which now shelled the holy city, had been sold to the Arabs by the Western powers, mainly the British.

Chief Rabbi Yitzhak Herzog at once dispatched a telegram of protest to the Pope, the United Nations, and the spiritual leaders of the superpowers. Although they expressed their "dismay," Christian leaders as a whole did not lift a finger to stop the bombardment.

A supply convoy on the road to Jerusalem in the spring of 1948.

of the shells exploded, it made a horrifying noise. But then, that was the main objective. The noise scared the Arabs so much that they called it "the Jews' atomic bomb." A few such Davidkas operated in Jerusalem, and to this day there is a special memorial erected in honor of the vital role played by the Davidkas in one of Jerusalem's central squares.

Ben-Gurion watched the situation closely. From time to time he traveled to Jerusalem in one of the convoys, or flew there in a light plane for crucial meetings with those in command of the city's defense. In his diary, he would express concern over the internal situation during the long siege. "The situation in Jerusalem is poor and dangerous," he wrote, or "The enemy is shelling the city day and night. Shells fall everywhere. Morale is bad. People cannot sleep. There is very little food. They have enough bread for only two more weeks, and that is all. Water is dished out in the streets; a half a can per person for two days. There are many seekers of peace—in other words, surrender . . . The poorer populations had fled the northern part of the city, afraid of the shelling."

On March 27, the Arabs destroyed an entire convoy en route to Jerusalem. On March 31, another Haganah convoy suffered very heavy casualties, and not a single vehicle reached Jerusalem.

Arab gangs controlled two vital points on the road to Jerusalem, at Shaar Hagai and Kastel. At times they fired on convoys from only a few yards away. The commander of the Arab bands was the highly regarded Abdul Khader al-Husseini, a cousin of the Mufti of Jerusalem.

Ben-Gurion ordered the launching of "Operation Nachshon" to cut through to Jerusalem. It proved to be one of the most difficult and crucial battles of the War of Independence, and it decided the fate of Jerusalem a month and a half before the birth of the State of Israel.

Artillery shells continued to rain on the city for weeks, one shell every two minutes. The Jews had nothing with which to return fire.

An invention by a young engineer named David Leibowitz came to their rescue; it was affectionately given his name—the "Davidka." It was a simple six-inch pipe from which he had made a mortar that fired shells containing nails and scrap metal. When one

A Jewish supply convoy is attacked on the road to Jerusalem in 1948.

Fifteen hundred Jewish fighters attacked on April 3. Ben-Gurion's order stated that wherever the British intervened, they were to be fought as well. The battles on the rocky slopes of the hills leading to Jerusalem, in which the fighters of the Palmach carried the main burden, were among the cruelest of the entire war. The Israeli offensive lasted a full week, and when the great victory finally came it was purely by chance.

Jewish fighters shot and killed three armed Arabs. When they checked the slain men, it turned out that one of the three was Abdul Khader, the most feared of Arab commanders. Thirty thousand Arabs participated in his funeral at the Dome of the Rock in the Temple Mount. Arab morale was dealt a crushing blow from which it never recovered.

The road to Jerusalem was opened—but only temporarily. A convoy of trucks filled with food left for Jerusalem at once on April 15. Two days later, 290 trucks with 950 tons of food—a convoy six miles long—reached Jerusalem. It arrived on the Sabbath, and even orthodox Jews left their synagogues to help in the unloading.

The Arabs, however, lay in wait for the third convoy at Shaar Hagai, which was still in their control, and opened concerted fire on its three hundred trucks. The battle lasted all day. Thirty Jews were wounded, three killed; six trucks went up in flames. To this day, their charred remains lie alongside the now wide and safe highway leading to Jerusalem via Shaar Hagai. The road to Jerusalem was then closed for seven weeks; the Holy City was completely cut off.

Ben-Gurion spent the Passover seder on April 22 with the besieged fighters of Jerusalem. Ben-Gurion felt that it was important that the residents of Jerusalem, and particularly the fighters, know that he was among them. The commanders of the Haganah, however, were against the idea. "We are totally opposed to your traveling to Jerusalem," they wrote. "There is no way of knowing when you will be able to return."

Ben-Gurion ignored them. This, too, was part of the secret of his leadership. He knew how to be in the right place at the right time.

Three days after the seder, Ben-Gurion managed to return to Tel Aviv in a light plane. "The flight lasted thirty-five minutes," Ben-Gurion wrote in his diary. "How small our country is!"

In the meantime, the Arab Legion had gained control of the Latrun police station and its surroundings. The Legion's armor and soldiers now blocked the road to Jerusalem. The justified feeling among the young officers of Israel's newly formed general staff was that the Legion had to be dislodged from Latrun or else the road to Jerusalem would remain blocked and the city would eventually fall due to lack of food and ammunition.

Ben-Gurion ordered an attack on the Arab Legion at Latrun during the night of May 24. "Jerusalem cannot be endangered," he said.

Ben-Gurion was encouraged by the first shipments of arms and aircraft now reaching Israel. The Security Council had accepted the Arabs' demand that the latest cease-fire be postponed for two days. Ben-Gurion feared the Arabs had called for the postponement in the hope that Jerusalem would fall during this brief period. So he ordered the Seventh Brigade to attack Latrun immediately and break through to Jerusalem. "Force, not U.N. decisions, will determine the fate of the country," he admonished those colleagues who opposed his plan.

But the attack on Latrun was a total failure. Israeli fighters set out from Kibbutz Hulda and stormed the Legion's positions but were thrown back, leaving behind them scores of dead and three hundred wounded. Ben-Gurion did not give up; he kept demanding that Latrun be taken, fearing the Arab Legion would attack Jerusalem.

Hundreds of recruits lacking military experience were thrown into the battle for Latrun. Some were sent to the battlefield straight from immigrant ships, which were now arriving openly in Israel. They were equipped with new weapons freshly arrived from Czechoslovakia.

But every assault failed. The battle for Latrun was the young Israeli Army's biggest failure in the War of Independence.

Among those who participated in the battle for Latrun during the brutally hot days of late May was a twenty-year-old Second Lieutenant named Ariel Scheinerman. During the preceding months, this young Haganah officer had fought the Arabs in the Sharon area near Kfar Malal, the moshav (communal farming village) in which he had been born. So fully engaged was he in fighting that he had not even managed to hear the radio broadcast of the declaration of statehood on May 15.

At Latrun he was in command of a company that stormed one of the Legion's strongholds. A number of his men were wounded and killed; he himself was wounded in the stomach and the leg. When the operation's command issued the order to withdraw,

Scheinerman was stuck with his men in a ravine; their canteens were empty, and his blood-smeared soldiers had to drink the putrid water in the ditch.

"He's gotten us out of every jam in the past," Scheinerman heard his soldiers whispering to each other behind his back. "Let's see him get us out of here."

Under the Legion's fire, and with superhuman effort, Ariel Scheinerman retreated with his men. The fire that spread in the field scorched the legs of the combatants, who were dressed in shorts and sandals. When the young officer awoke, he found himself in a hospital. Years later, after he had become known as General Ariel Sharon, he said to me: "During those bitter hours of that terrible day on the battlefield of Latrun, I swore to myself that in all future encounters between ourselves and the Arabs, we must always emerge victorious."

King Abdullah

BEN-GURION tried until the last minute to avert war with at least one Arab state, Transjordan. He dispatched a secret emissary to meet with King Abdullah just a few days prior to the establishment of the Jewish state. Ben-Gurion wanted to reach an agreement with Abdullah to keep the Arab Legion, the most effective Arab force, out of the war with Israel. The Legion's commander was Sir John Glubb, a British officer known to the Arabs as Glubb Pasha.

Ben-Gurion also tried to come to agreement with Egypt's King Farouk. A courageous Jewish woman, Yolanda Harmer, who worked secretly for the Haganah in Cairo, tried in vain to organize confidential meetings between the King and Ben-Gurion's emissaries.

The climax of Ben-Gurion's desperate attempts were his efforts over many years to

King Abdullah, grandfather of Jordan's present King, with his officers.

171

reach an accord for the peaceful coexistence of a Jewish and Arab state. But the Arabs were unwilling to allow the Jews even the small slice the United Nations had apportioned them.

The Palestinians committed a fundamental historic error (from their point of view), one they have continued to make for many years since; an error that has not only prevented them from gaining an independent state of their own, but which also led to Israel expanding her territory. For thirty years, to this day, King Hussein has continued the ongoing secret contacts with Israeli leaders begun by his grandfather, Abdullah. No peace, however, has resulted from these endless talks.

In 1948, Ben-Gurion sent Golda Meir to meet with Abdullah in a last-minute attempt to limit the magnitude of the inevitable Arab offensive. Ben-Gurion implicitly trusted this dynamic woman who had been his loyal ally through all his political battles.

Golda, then in her fifties, had traveled a long and difficult Zionist path. Born in Kiev, she had as a child witnessed Cossack pogroms against Jews. Her terrifying childhood memories never left her.

Together with hundreds of thousands of other Eastern European Jews who sought security and economic prosperity in the New World, Golda's family emigrated to the United States. But though Golda grew up in Milwaukee and married at the age of nineteen, she became a zealous activist in one of the Zionist socialist organizations. The enthusiasm created by the 1917 Balfour Declaration, which committed Britain to a homeland for the Jews in Eretz Yisrael, led to Golda's decision to immigrate there. Even the distressing news of forty Jews killed and wounded by Arabs in protest against the Balfour Declaration did not deter her. That same month, Golda set sail for Eretz Yisrael and became an inseparable part of Israeli history from that time on; the leading woman in a small team

of tough men who conducted the crucial stage of the struggle for independence.

In March 1947 Ben-Gurion sent Golda to the United States to raise funds from the Jewish community for the purchase of desperately needed arms. When she returned with the enormous sum of fifty million dollars, Ben Gurion remarked, "Someday, when the history of the State of Israel is written, it will be noted that it was a Jewish woman who raised the money that made the establishment of the state possible."

Now Ben-Gurion asked Golda, then serving as head of the Jewish Agency's Political Department, to meet with Abdullah once more. She first met the Jordanian in November 1947 at a house overlooking the Jordan River. The King, who had long maintained contacts with various Jews, promised Golda he would always remain a friend to the Jews and would not support any attack against them. The Jews, he believed, would bring progress and economic development to the entire Mideast. The principles of the agreement worked out by Ben-Gurion and the King suggested that the latter would place the area of the proposed Arab state under his rule, leaving the Jews alone, so they hoped, to establish a state of their own.

Now, however, after the Partition Plan resolution and the bloody riots in Eretz Yisrael, Golda feared he would join the Arab rejectionist front. Abdullah tried to calm her, sending a confidential message: "As a Bedouin, my word is my bond. As a King, my word of honor is doublefold. And above all, I would never break a promise I have given to a woman."

Even this gentlemanly chivalry did not placate Ben-Gurion and Golda. They wanted a clear answer: would Abdullah's Arab Legion go to war against Israel?

Therefore, Golda set out on a mission to see the King, traveling on roads beset with Arab gangs. She arrived at Abdullah's palace in Amman at midnight, May 10, disguised in the dress and dark scarves of a Muslim woman, and driven in a car with blacked-out windows and curtains.

The King, pale and tense, received her. He would not be able to keep his promise, Abdullah carefully explained, because of his obligations to Egypt, Syria, Lebanon, and Iraq. "I am no longer the master of my destiny," the King told Golda.

The King then made a proposal of his own: that the Jews refrain from hurrying to declare their independence. It would be better he felt, if they deferred this for a few years, and also put a stop to all immigration. In the meantime, he would take control of the entire country and allow the Jews representation in his Parliament.

"A people who have waited two thousand years for this day cannot be described as being in a hurry," Golda replied tersely. "We don't want war, but in view of what you have said, it appears that war will break out—and we will be the victors."

Golda was accompanied by Ben-Gurion's adviser for Arab affairs, Ezra Danin, who knew Abdullah well. "You rely too heavily on your tanks" he told the King. "You have no true friends in the Arab world, and we will destroy your tanks just as the Maginot Line was shattered [during World War II along the French-German border]."

"Our fate is in the hands of Allah," Abdullah replied sadly.

Three years later in 1951, Abdullah was assassinated by his Arab foes on the steps of Al-Aksa Mosque on Jerusalem's Temple Mount, where he had come to pray. They accused him of being a "Zionist agent." Thirty years after that, Sadat was assassinated in Cairo for signing a peace treaty with Israel. Nonetheless, Abdullah's grandson, Hussein, continued to hold secret meetings with Israelis, even after 1967, when he lost the West Bank his grandfather had left him.

Golda Meir, dispatched by Ben-Gurion to ensure the neutrality of King Abdullah.

Golda gave a detailed report to Ben-Gurion after her meeting with the King. She had no doubt Abdullah would join the fighting, and that this would increase by thousands the number of Jewish casualties, "There will be a war," Golda told Ben-Gurion, "and not only will the Jordanians join in, but the Iraqis too. Through the windows of my car, I saw Jordanian and Iraqi soldiers and vehicles amassed on the roads."

Ben-Gurion understood the dramatic meaning of this message. His worst fears would be realized—there would be war with seven regular Arab armies.

In his diary, Ben-Gurion writes that immediately after hearing Golda's report, he called in his senior military advisers and demanded that they "prepare for battle against an all-out Arab invasion force." He also instructed that all Jewish forces be turned into mobile units. And above all, they should "open the road to Jerusalem and its hundred thousand Jews, who are surrounded by heavily populated Arab villages. Weapons and reinforcements must be sent there." On the eve of the proclamation of statehood, Ben-Gurion foresaw that the battle for Jerusalem would be the focal point of the war—militarily, historically, and in terms of morale.

As if to prove that Abdullah had meant what he said, the Legion attacked the 550 defenders in the four kibbutzim of Gush Etzion with tanks and a force of 1,500 men. These settlements, which controlled the road to Jerusalem, fell in two days.

On the afternoon of May 12, Ben-Gurion convened a fateful meeting. The only question on the agenda was whether Israel should declare independence on the very day the British were scheduled to leave Jerusalem. Under American pressure, the United Nations had proposed that all sides agree to a cease-fire and that the Jews postpone the establishment of their state. Ten of the thirteen members of the Provisional People's Council participated in a dramatic debate presided over by Ben-Gurion. Four supported the U.N. proposal. Ben-Gurion, one of the six who rejected it, decided that independence would be declared two days later, on Friday, at four P.M.

Ben-Gurion was the driving force behind this decision. It would have been easy to accept the cease-fire proposal and postpone the proclamation of the state. Jerusalem was under siege, Gush Etzion was collapsing, and the Arab armies were massing for invasion. Why not accept a cease-fire?

Ben-Gurion's great sense of statesmanship told him that if he did not declare independence at the time appointed, there might never be another opportunity to do so. This was a crucial moment, a turning point in Jewish history not to be missed. All ears were tuned to Ben-Gurion; everyone was awaiting his decision. If he had said "postpone independence," they would have accepted it.

The Jewish population had prepared the tools. It had built cities, kibbutzim, and moshavim, had set up a shadow army and prepared weapons. But someone had to make the decision. There were many Jews who feared they would be unable to hold out against the Arab armies; it was a race against time. The British had succeeded, on the eve of their departure, in creating chaos in the Holy Land. The Haganah, at this stage, possessed not a single tank; its forces numbered but forty-five thousand men and women, whose primary weapons were rifles, Sten submachine guns, and light machine guns.

On the face of things, it appeared that Ben-Gurion had taken a tremendous gamble with the fate of the entire Yishuv. But he was a man who did more than speak of spirit—he created it; he knew it existed. He perceived it in the battles that had been waged for the previous six months.

At the appointed hour of four P.M., he arrived at the ceremony in a dark suit. "Jewish Independence was declared and the State of Israel was established," he wrote in his diary that night. "Will Tel Aviv be bombed tonight?"

On the morning of May 15, five Egyptian planes bombed Tel Aviv, inflicting dozens of casualties. That same day, President Harry Truman recognized the government of Israel; his action was followed three days later by recognition from Moscow. It was virtually the only time the United States and U.S.S.R. agreed on something throughout the Cold War of the late 1940s and '50s.

Independence

The Old City

IF THERE WAS one thing that shocked and appalled the Jews in the new state, it was the fall of the Jewish Quarter of the Old City—including the Western Wall—into Arab hands. Ben-Gurion ordered that all efforts be made to stop the Arabs from taking the quarter. On April 6 he explained that "the value of Jerusalem cannot be measured, weighed, or counted. Because if a nation has a soul, Jerusalem is the soul of Eretz Yisrael. The battle for Jerusalem is decisive, not just militarily. . . . The ancient pledge, 'By the rivers of Babylon, [there we sat down, yea, we wept when we remembered Zion],' is as binding today as it was then . . ."

On the morning of Friday, May 14, the British evacuated Jerusalem, one day earlier than planned and thirty years after British forces under General Allenby had liberated the city from the Turks. Both sides, the Haganah and the Arabs, moved quickly to take

Jews in Jerusalem capitulating to the Arab Legion in May 1948.

Jewish defenders of the Old City of Jerusalem at the end of May 1948.

control of key positions that the British had vacated without notifying the Jews.

The Israeli commander in Jerusalem, David Shaltiel, had to ask the Chief Rabbis—including the father of Israel's current President, Chaim Herzog—for special dispensation to allow the Jews to work on Old City fortifications on the Sabbath. Old men and children were enlisted for the task. Shaltiel patrolled between the lines in order to supervise the construction. Suddenly he noticed an elderly Jew pushing a large stone. He was stunned to see that it was Rabbi Uziel, the Sephardic Chief Rabbi. "Honorable Rabbi, what are you doing here?" he asked. "After all, this is not

your job." The rabbi looked at him and said, "If the Jews don't see that I too am working on the Sabbath, they may not believe that violating the sanctity of the Sabbath today is actually sanctifying the Sabbath."

But while the Jews gained control of key points in the New City, the situation in the Jewish Quarter of the Old City continued to deteriorate. Forces of the Arab Legion and units of the Egyptian Army prepared to advance with the clear intention of preventing the internationalization of the Holy City, as provided by the United Nations resolution.

Ben-Gurion foresaw the course of events clearly. On May 19 he wrote in his diary: "We must move quickly to defeat two generals threatening Jerusalem: hunger and the Legion."

Hunger could be conquered only by opening the road to Jerusalem, so the Arab Legion would have to be stopped in the city itself. King Abdullah knew that by taking Jerusalem, he would become a most important Arab leader, "the Defender of Jerusalem," rather than just a Bedouin king. The Legion, the best army in the Middle East, commanded by British officers and equipped with armored cars, cannon, and mortars, prepared to advance.

When Yitzhak Rabin, the brilliant young Palmach officer fighting in the hills of Jerusalem, asked Ben-Gurion, "What comes first, Jerusalem or the road?" Ben-Gurion answered, to the point: "Both!" Rabin was in command of the Palmach's Harel Brigade, which had been fighting to open the road to Jerusalem and stop Arab forces from breaking into the city. The Harel Brigade was now assigned the task of moving into the Old City.

All Jerusalem was under siege, the road to the city being cut off. The Jewish Quarter, however, was the subject of a siege within a siege that had begun in December 1947. The fifteen hundred Jews—all but three hundred of them old men, women, and children—who had lived for generations in impoverished homes near the remains of the Temple were surrounded by twenty thousand Arabs, mostly armed. The entire Jewish Quarter covered an area only 400 yards long and 300 yards wide. The Western Wall was 150 yards from the closest Jewish courtyard.

The British made sure that no fighters or weapons were allowed into the Jewish Quarter, though the Arabs were allowed free access to the Old City. Most of the Jews who walked through the winding narrow alleys of the Jewish Quarter were rabbis and yeshiva students engaged in the study of the Torah. Two particularly ancient synagogues were located

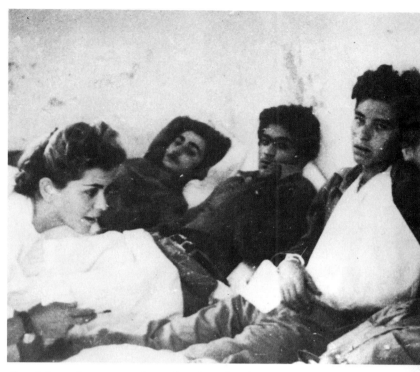

Jewish prisoners after the battle for Jerusalem.

there: the Synagogue of Rabbi Yochanan Ben Zakkai and the Hurvah, the synagogue of Rabbi Yehuda He-Hasid, which was the central Ashkenazi place of worship.

By bribing British soldiers, the Haganah succeeded in sneaking small groups of fighters and a few arms into the Old City. The Arabs refused to allow food into the Jewish Quarter, but the Jews managed to force the British into ensuring a meager provision of food supplies.

The religious Jews of the Jewish Quarter did not approve of the mostly nonreligious young Jews, without beards and earlocks, who had come to protect them. The majority of the religious Jews did not care who ruled Jerusalem, as long as they could continue praying at the Western Wall. The Haganah, however, were determined to ensure that when the State of Israel was established, it would be in control of the Wall.

On May 13 a British officer appeared at the home of Rabbi Mordechai Weingarten, head of the Jewish community, and politely told

Scenes from the fall of the Old City of Jerusalem.

him that the British were leaving the Old City. He handed him the key to the Zion Gate, saying, "Since the year seventy, the keys of Jerusalem have not been in the hands of Jews. Now, after eighteen hundred years, they are finally in your hands."

Fifteen days later, Israel would learn the bitter lesson: It had won the keys, but not the city.

On May 18 the Arabs began storming the Jewish Quarter. The defenders called on command headquarters, located in the New City, for help. They needed more men, weapons, and food. They already knew of the fall of Gush Etzion and the massacre that had been perpetrated there. An Arab broadcast that once the Jews surrendered they "should all be stood up against the wall in order to teach them a lesson" had been recorded by command headquarters.

As the Arab bombardment began, the Jews left their homes and took refuge in underground shelters in synagogues and in basements of stone houses. Many of the Jews gathered in one of the Old City's synagogues and began praying. They heard the Arabs' loudspeakers in the background calling on them in both Hebrew and Arabic to surrender. A message sent to King Abdullah by the attacking forces was also intercepted: "Two companies have attacked the Jewish Quarter in the Old City. We are winning, thanks to the artillery bombardment."

The 150 Jewish fighters knew that the time for prayer had already passed. They tried to stop the Arabs at all costs. If wounded, they would return to their posts after receiving first aid. There is a well-known story of a young man who was hit in the eye by shrapnel. When told that medical treatment would take a quarter of an hour, he asked that they just put drops in his eye. "The situation at my post is bad, and I must return," he said. An hour later a shell shattered his head.

Synagogues became hospitals; their wooden benches, beds. The Talmud was taken off the shelves and replaced by rolls of bandages.

In a primitive workshop, fighters made hand grenades and bombs: explosives placed in tin cans. Women were asked to gather old tin cans and containers. Orthodox women emptied coffee and tea cans and gave them to the fighters, along with a prayer: "May it be God's will that my bomb throws back the enemy and forces him to leave our Holy City." Other women gathered matches to light the explosives. Young children served as communications messengers, running between bombarded positions in order to convey orders and bring the bullets and homemade hand grenades.

The moment of truth was approaching. Headquarters in the New City promised help, but it never arrived. Shaltiel had gained his thorough military experience during the 1920s as a sergeant in the French Foreign Legion. He was a brave commander who defended the New City throughout the siege, but he did not have sufficient forces to begin a counteroffensive in the Old City.

The Arabs penetrated the Jewish Quarter and began demolishing house after house. Their advance was slow because they would stop to loot each house before destroying it. Some of the Jews were broken in spirit and ran out with a white flag of surrender.

During the night of May 18 an ear-shattering explosion startled all of Jerusalem: A Palmach unit had succeeded in blowing its way through the Zion Gate and quickly covered the 150 yards to the Jewish Quarter. Some of the defenders, who had been in the Old City for four months, were replaced, but many chose to stay on and fight. Some supplies, including cases of ammunition and medical equipment, were brought in.

The Israelis, however, were unable to protect the breach in the Old City's sixteenth-century wall. Their military experience was limited, and they failed to understand that they had to hold this opening at all costs, despite heavy casualties. They did not understand that the breach that night was the only possible route by which the Old City could have been saved.

The breach in the wall was quickly closed by an Arab counterattack, and the fate of the Jewish Quarter was sealed. At nine o'clock on the morning of May 19 the Arab Legion re-captured the Zion Gate. The siege of the Jewish Quarter had been resumed.

While the bitter battle was being fought in the Old City, serious difficulties divided the newborn state's military leadership. Ben-Gurion issued orders, but they were not always carried out. David Shaltiel, who had succeeded in defending the New City, differed with the Palmach over the defense of the Old City and Jerusalem as a whole.

The true reason for their disagreement was actually the difference in mentality between Shaltiel and the Palmach. The commanders of the Palmach represented the spirit of the new semipartisan, volunteer Israeli Army. Shaltiel was, in their eyes, a symbol of the tough military commander, a man of iron discipline and a military "square." In the controversy over who was responsible for the fall of the Old City, David Shaltiel became perhaps the most tragic figure in the fight for Jerusalem.

Shaltiel, who as commander of the Jerusalem District* was given the rank of general, was born to a Portuguese Jewish family in Hamburg, Germany. As a young man he left home and immigrated to Eretz Yisrael, working as a waiter at a hotel in the Old City. In 1926 he traveled to France and decided to enlist in the Foreign Legion. He served five years, mostly in the North African desert, receiving a medal of bravery for his part in the battles against Abd-el-Krim, leader of the Rif revolt in Morocco.

After his discharge from the Foreign Legion in 1931, he went to live in Paris, where he worked for the Shell Oil Company and met a young French widow, Léonie Boudieu. Together they moved to Metz in 1933, after Shaltiel was appointed Shell's representative in the Alsace region. He spoke fluent French and German and enjoyed the affluent middle-class life there.

---

* The "Jerusalem District" refers to the entire city of Jerusalem and the adjacent areas.

He was happy in Metz—until he met the first Jewish refugees from Nazi persecution. Their stories shocked him. Then he attended a lecture in Metz by a Haganah representative entitled "Quo Vadis Judaeus?" ("Where Are You Going, O Jew?").

Shaltiel first left Metz for Paris to become involved in Zionist immigration to Eretz Yisrael. A short while later he himself became one of those immigrants, together with a different woman, Inge, whom he married. In 1935 Shaltiel was sent back to Paris by the Haganah on a secret mission of arms purchases. In 1936 he once again returned to Eretz Yisrael, where he was given a command in the Haganah. In 1936, on a new mission for the Haganah in Europe, he was arrested by the Nazi Gestapo and, although acquitted in a trial, was sent to the concentration camps of Dachau and Buchenwald. On March 18, 1939, he was released by the Germans and returned to Palestine, where he progressed in the command echelons of the Haganah and in February 1948 was appointed commander of the Jerusalem District by Ben-Gurion.

During the last days of May 1948 Shaltiel had to defend all of Jewish-held Jerusalem from attacks by the Jordanian and Egyptian armies and thousands of armed Arab irregulars surrounding the city. Receiving desperate messages from the Old City that "we will be slaughtered in a matter of hours," he demanded that the Palmach break into the Old City, hold the bridgehead, and transfer forces to the Jewish Quarter. The Palmachniks, however, claimed that their role was limited to breaking through and that it was up to Shaltiel to find others to defend the bridgehead and reinforce the Jewish Quarter.

The historic controversy surrounding this argument has not been resolved to this day and has generated conflicting accusations. The fact is, however, that from the time of the successful breakthrough at the Zion Gate, all other attempts to link up with the besieged Jewish Quarter failed. Desperate and at times hysterical communications were received from the Jewish Quarter, a distance of only a few hundred yards from where Jews on the other side of the wall stood by helplessly. The ratio between the attacking Arab forces and the Jewish defenders was twenty to one, and behind the attackers were thousands of additional Arabs demanding the slaughter of every Jew in the Old City. Individual Jewish fighters set the terrible tone of the battle, which has been compared to the Jewish uprising in the Warsaw Ghetto during World War II. The Jewish fighters in the Old City would mount surprise attacks on bands of Arabs and kill or wound them in order to seize their weapons and continue fighting. The feeling that they were defending the very heart of Jerusalem led the combatants to acts of desperate bravery. Shaltiel implored them to hold on, promising that help would come.

On May 20 the fighters in the Old City notified Shaltiel that they had only a hundred hand grenades left. They requested that ammunition be dropped to them by air, but this proved to be impossible. A Reuters correspondent accompanying the Arab Legion wrote: "The soldiers of the Arab Legion had to inch their way forward step by step, setting off explosions, in order to reach the Jewish suicide squads who continued their resistance from mounds of rubble inside the Jewish Quarter of the Old City." On May 22 the Arab Legion broke into the Tiferet Yisrael Synagogue and the battle seemed to be over. But the brave defenders continued their stand, using their few weapons sparingly but effectively while slowly retreating. On three separate occasions they were notified from the outside, "Tonight we will be breaking through to you," but they were always disappointed. They continued fighting for every house, every courtyard, every corner.

Finally they gathered in the only building still standing, the Hurvah Synagogue. The

Legion had no qualms about bombarding and capturing this site—next to the Wall, the holiest site to the Orthodox Jews of Jerusalem—and flying its flag over it. With the conquest of the Hurvah, the Arabs reached the center of the Jewish Quarter.

On May 28 Israeli soldiers at an observation point on Mount Zion were shocked to see their Jewish brethren in the Old City surrendering: a group of elderly Jews and a young girl in a nurse's uniform, white flags in their hands, walking by the Zion Gate under the escort of Arab Legion military police. The civilian population had demanded the surrender. The rabbis came out with a white flag and were brought before the commander of the Arab Legion in the Old City, Abdullah El-Tal, who dictated the terms of surrender.

When the soldiers of the Arab Legion saw that the remaining Jewish defenders of the Old City numbered only forty fighters with a meager pile of arms, they burst out in cries of fury, "Dogs! If only we had known, we would have attacked you with sticks alone!" It turned out that the Jewish defenders had but a hundred rifles, five machine guns, fifty-four submachine guns, two mortars, and five thousand 9-mm bullets. In the last two weeks of the siege six Jews were killed and two hundred wounded.

The Arabs pillaged and destroyed all twenty-seven synagogues in the Old City. Prayerbooks were burned and Jewish homes destroyed. The area surrounding the Temple Mount had known previous Jewish surrenders. This, however, was the first time in history that their surrender did not determine the Jews' political fate. They held the New City of Jerusalem. Nonetheless, it was a severe blow to Jewish morale. For many years they would describe the fall of the Old City and the Western Wall as a "disaster for generations."

Just nineteen years later, when King Hussein, Abdullah's grandson, made the mistake of his life and joined Egypt and Syria in the Six-Day War, Israel liberated the Old City and the Western Wall. Since then the Jewish Quarter has been rebuilt.

On the very day in June 1967 that Israel liberated the Old City, David Shaltiel quickly made his way to the Western Wall together with thousands who were congregating there. When he entered the Old City through the Zion Gate, few recognized him as the commander of Jerusalem during the War of Independence. He arrived at the Western Wall and stood there, his eyes flooding with tears. The former sergeant in the French Foreign Legion, the general in Jerusalem, stood there like an excited child.

Shaltiel now felt he could write his own story of the war for Jerusalem in 1948. He made an appointment to meet with Larry Collins and Dominique Lapierre, who wanted to interview him for their book *O Jerusalem*. But on February 23, 1969, one month before their appointed meeting, he died in Jerusalem.

The Arab Invasion

AT ONE MINUTE past midnight on May 15, 1948—less than eight hours after David Ben-Gurion had proclaimed the State of Israel— tens of thousands of Egyptian soldiers crossed the border. Moving quickly over the desert roads, they arrived in Gaza later that day. In the Negev, Egyptian artillery launched attacks against kibbutzim.

It was the first day of the first of the wars between Egypt and the Jewish state, conflicts that would not end until March 1979, when Egypt became the first Arab state to make peace with its Jewish neighbors.

That same night of May 14/15 the Syrians shelled the entire length of their frontier with Israel with artillery barrages. Infantry and armored vehicles, supported by aviation and artillery, sped toward the kibbutzim of the Jordan Valley. Armored units of the Lebanese

Israeli fighters at the front in May 1948. On May 15, 1948, seven Arab armies attacked the State of Israel.

185

*Arab fighters at the front near Kibbutz Mishmar Haemek, northern
Israel, May 1948.*

Army invaded Upper Galilee. An Iraqi Expeditionary Corps, equipped with heavy armaments, also crossed the Jordan, as did the Arab Redemption Army. Most important, the well-trained Arab Legion attacked Jerusalem, supported by Egyptian units, for King Farouk hoped to share the crown of Jerusalem with Transjordan's Abdullah.

Thus, in the first few hours of its birth, the Jewish state was attacked from three directions: south, north, and east. Under the invasion plan, the Syrians and Lebanese were to break through as far as the center of Galilee and meet up with the Jordanian and Iraqi forces in order to conquer Haifa by May 20—five days away. The Egyptians were to reach

Tel Aviv by May 25, after destroying the settlements in the Negev. The Arab Legion entered Samaria and, after sending a key force to Latrun, slipped into East Jerusalem. The Iraqi Army had also moved into Samaria to back up the Legion in the battle for Jerusalem, which was scheduled to fall at the same time as Tel Aviv.

Some of the Arab inroads were impressive; in the first few weeks the Egyptians came within twenty miles of Tel Aviv; units of the Legion actually came even closer. Their clear objective was to strangle the state in its infancy, using the superior numbers of the Arab regular forces.

The Egyptian Army, with 45,000 troops,

Kibbutz Negba following the raid by the Egyptian Air Force, August 1948.

The first female recruits in the Israeli Army, 1948.

*Entrenched fighters
battling it out in 1948.*

The Arab Legion in Jerusalem.

The Mufti of Jerusalem with Arab troops.

Sir John Glubb—Glubb Pasha (left), commander of the Arab Legion, with al-Jundi, his second in command, and Azzam Pasha, Secretary of the Arab League.

A Haganah camp: scouts from a neighboring kibbutz reporting enemy troop movements.

Israeli offensive in Galilee (above) and in the Negev (below).

was equipped with modern weapons, which themselves outnumbered those of the Yishuv, whose limited arms were also obsolete. Cairo's air force possessed 10 squadrons, 8 of them combat, with 200 pilots. Its navy included 2 warships, 2 transport ships, and 4 police coastal patrol boats. On top of all that, the Egyptians had tanks, batteries of cannon, and mortars.

Syria's army numbered 11,800 troops, plus a motorized battalion, several thousand cavalry, tanks, and cannon batteries. The Lebanese military's 5,500 soldiers were split into 4 infantry battalions, one artillery battalion, and one motorized company. The Iraqis invaded with 35,000 well-armed infantry and artillery soldiers. Iraq's air force possessed several squadrons of interceptors. Transjordan's army was made up of 18,000 men, led by British officers and accompanied by 50 cannons and 400 armored vehicles. And the Saudis pos-

sessed a regular army of 25,000 men plus a tribal militia of 12,000.*

The Arab states, on the eve of the invasion, had at their disposal over 100,000 troops and modern weaponry.

Against this impressive array stood the forces of the Yishuv, most of them used only

* The Saudi task force was made up of three battalions, integrated on the Egyptian battlefront. With the exception of the Suez crisis of 1956 and the Israeli war in Lebanon in 1982, Saudi forces have been involved in all wars waged by the Arabs against Israel.

Israeli soldiers digging in with an anti-aircraft weapon.

to fighting in small clandestine units. The regular army—not even officially created until ten days after the outbreak of the war—was composed of but 16,500 soldiers; to this were added 13,500 kibbutz and moshav members with weapons experience: in all, just 30,000 soldiers.

Ben-Gurion named the new Jewish army the Israel Defense Forces (IDF), both to underline its link with the Haganah and to stress that the army was not created for offensive purposes. He hoped Menachem Begin's Irgun would join its ranks, but was to be disappointed.

So concerned was the new Prime Minister about the arms situation that he anxiously counted each plane arriving from Czechoslovakia. "One more Messerschmidt arrived this evening," he recorded in his diary on May 23, 1948. "It's armed with two cannon and bombs. Tomorrow we will have two Messerschmidts ready for action."

By the end of the first month of the war the IDF had mobilized 41,000 fighters in 12 brigades. Most of the fighters were new immigrants, fresh off the boat; many could not even speak Hebrew.

Three of the brigades were composed of Palmach veterans, the Yishuv's military elite, commanded by such well-known officers as Yitzhak Sadeh, Yigal Allon, and Yitzhak Rabin. It was largely with these troops that Ben-Gurion conducted the War of Independence.

An Israeli armored convoy on the road to Jerusalem.

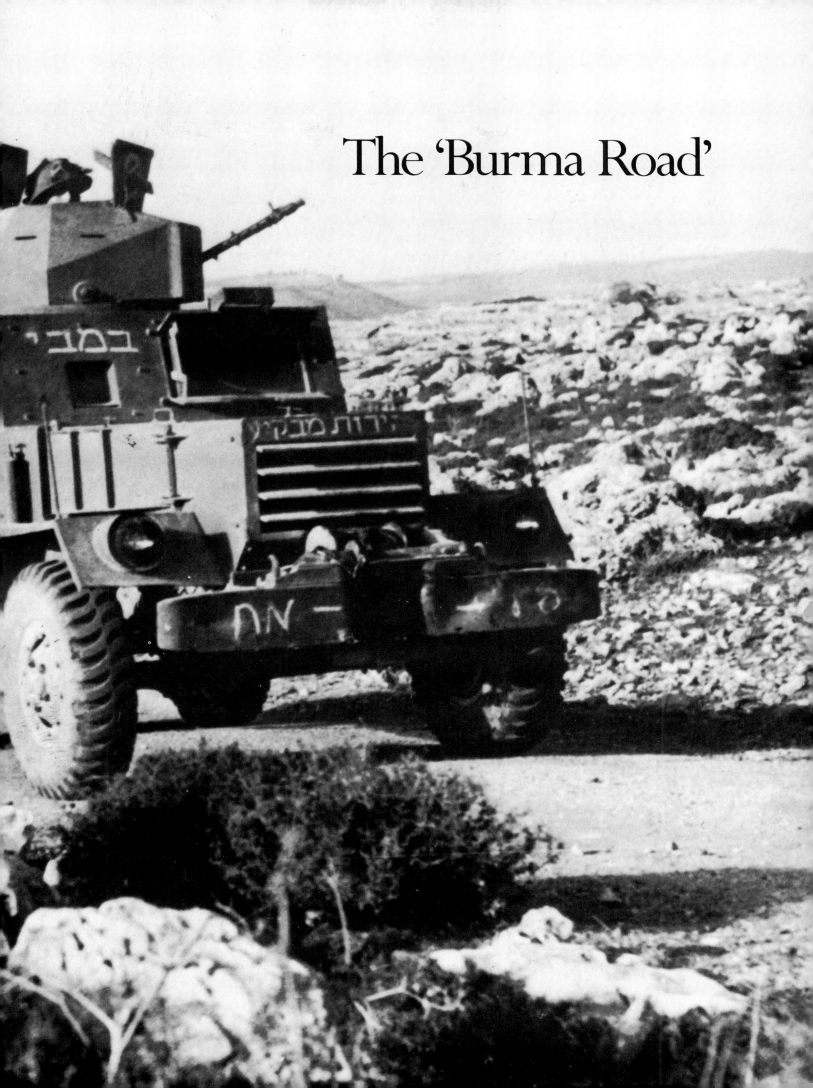

The 'Burma Road'

IN JERUSALEM strict food and gasoline rationing and incessant shelling combined to produce an atmosphere in which often contradictory rumors were rife, causing people to pass in turn from hope to despair. The repeated failure of Israeli attacks against the Arab Legion at Latrun had sent a wave of pessimism over Jerusalem. The mood grew worse as the road to the city remained closed.

Jerusalem was, from the start, surrounded on all sides by mountains populated by Arab villages. The villagers, later reinforced by the Arab Legion, besieged the city. The only artery capable of keeping life going in Jerusalem was the road leading west, connecting the city with Tel Aviv and the coastal plain, which was controlled by the Jews. The main problem confronting the Jews during the crucial battle for Jerusalem was how to keep this road open. The road itself wound through mountainous terrain, threatened by the Arabs, via Shaar Hagai and Latrun. With Transjordan's Arab Legion controlling Latrun, the road to Jerusalem—and the pipeline for Jewish survival in the city—was blocked.

At the end of May 1948, however, an optimistic whisper was spread that a new path had been opened, the "Burma Road," as it became known. It was this road that helped save Jerusalem.

The route was found by pure chance. According to one story, the idea first arose when a jeep full of soldiers coming from Hulda lost its way and managed to reach Shaar Hagai via two small Arab villages south of Latrun, Beit Jeez and Beit Sussin, which had been captured by the Israelis. The route taken by the jeeps proved that the Legion's strongholds at Latrun could be bypassed and that the road to Jerusalem could be reached via a roundabout path south of Latrun.

This was one of the greatest Jewish operations in the course of the battle for Jerusalem. The Jews immediately began cutting the new road. Although the stretch from Shaar Hagai to Jerusalem was already more or less in Israeli hands, topographical factors and the

Soldier of the Palmach, the shock troops of the Israeli Army, in the Negev, 1948.

The Burma Road in June 1948: Tractors towed armored vehicles up the steep hills.

threat posed by the Arab Legion from Latrun made it imperative for the Jews to carve a road from near the Israeli kibbutz of Hulda, climbing to the deserted Arab village of Saris. There the bypass linked up with the road to the Holy City. However, the mile-and-a-half stretch south of Shaar Hagai did not contain so much as a path or trail to enable the Israelis to avail themselves of this newfound route. What was more, the steep grade, strewn with enormous boulders, made it essential to bring in a bulldozer to clear the way for the supply trucks coming from Tel Aviv, via Hulda.

The scarcity of food in besieged Jerusalem had reached critical proportions. To alleviate the situation as much as conditions allowed before the road could be built, the Israelis brought in supplies on forty pack mules. At the point where even the mules could go no farther on the rough mountainous terrain below Jerusalem, two hundred volunteers, some of them fifty years old or more, took over. Each carried a forty-four-pound sack of flour on his back over the three-mile stretch leading to Jerusalem. Despite continued mortar fire from Latrun, these brave men doggedly stuck to their task night after night until the full complement of supplies had been ferried to their locked-in city.

Meanwhile, over a period of six weeks, the bulldozers cleared an easier road. Hundreds of the inhabitants of Jerusalem who were experts in stone quarrying worked night after night on the preparation of this vital portion of the road. This enabled trucks, with the aid of tractors, to climb to the crest of the hill. To speed the flow of gasoline to the city, the Jews laid a pipe directly to tankers parked below. All this was done under cover, to keep the new road secret as long as possible.

In this way the Israelis circumvented the well-fortified Arab Legion positions at Latrun —positions from which the Legion troops were not dislodged until 1967.

Among the commanders of the battle for Jerusalem was David (Mickey) Marcus of Brooklyn, a West Point–trained U.S. Army colonel and the highest-ranking foreign volunteer in the Jewish forces. His presence in Palestine was kept secret and he operated under the alias of "Stone." But that didn't keep Ben-Gurion from appointing him the first general of a Jewish army since Bar Kochba led the Jewish revolt against the Romans in the first century.

Tragically, Marcus was killed accidentally by one of his own troops who failed to recognize him walking alone at dawn. So distressed was Ben-Gurion by his death that he dispatched Moshe Dayan and Yossi Harel—in the middle of the war—to accompany his body to its final resting place in West Point, where he is the only person buried who was killed fighting under a foreign flag.

From June 1948 until the end of the War of Independence, the Burma Road served as Jerusalem's lifeline. Ben-Gurion would later comment on this road: "This was the climax of our war effort for our own homeland and our independence, because it is inseparably connected with our struggle for Jerusalem. This was the focal point of the War of Independence."

The fight for Jerusalem went on unabated. Ben-Gurion recorded in his diary: "The heavy shellings continue. The inability to respond in the same terms is very depressing. If only we had one heavy weapon in the city, this would alter the bleak mood of helplessness. People from the Mea Shearim quarter [the ultra-Orthodox section] detach themselves completely and don't lift a finger to help. They don't enlist in the struggle, yet they suffer more than others from the constant shooting— what is more, there is an air of defeatism in that quarter. . . ."

An even more complex problem was the supply of water to Jerusalem. The U.N. demanded that the Arabs restore the flow of water to Jerusalem, but lengthy negotiations made it clear the Arabs hoped to evade the issue. They effectively exploited the facts that the pumping station near Latrun was in the hands of the Arab Legion and that the waterworks at Rosh Ha'ayin were held by an Iraqi unit. It thus became necessary to hold separate talks with the Legion and with the Iraqis.

In the end, the supply of water to the Holy City was not restored. Only thanks to the frugal and organized allocation of water did the Jews of Jerusalem hold out during the scorching months of the summer of 1948.

The Early Days
of the Air Force

THE FIRST Egyptian plane shot down in the War of Independence was brought down over Tel Aviv on May 15, 1948. While other planes hit a synagogue and bombed the power station in north Tel Aviv, an Egyptian Spitfire ditched into the sea, just off the beach. That same day the Israelis quickly pulled the wreckage out of the water and discovered that they were able to refit it to make it airworthy.

Before an Israel-Egypt peace treaty, signed some thirty years later by Menachem Begin and Anwar al-Sadat, could be formulated at Camp David in September 1978, it was necessary for the Israeli Air Force to shoot down hundreds of Egyptian planes, mostly Soviet-made. The Israeli Air Force became recognized as one of the finest in the world.

But in May 1948 the Israelis had nothing even approaching an air force. All they had was a few light single-engine planes which, among other things, also served as "bombers." The pilot, or someone with him in the plane, would hurl bombs or grenades at the advancing Arabs. These small planes flew many dan-

gerous missions, airlifting food and weapons to cut-off areas in the Negev and Galilee. Operations of this sort began even under the noses of the British, who were busy packing to leave Palestine. But the Israelis did not have any means of intercepting Egyptian planes or of bombing any of the Arab capitals.

However, the Israelis did have some pilots of their own, inexperienced though they may have been: young Israelis who had trained with the British Royal Air Force in the Second World War. One of them—a charming young man with a sharp tongue and quick wit who had volunteered for the Royal Air Force —was Ezer Weizman, whose uncle, Chaim Weizmann, had become the leader of the Zionist movement in the years of struggle against the British. In 1948 Weizman, popular with women and possessed of a rare sense of humor, became one of the Israeli Air Force's first combat pilots. But even Weizman, with his rich imagination, could hardly conceive then that ten years later he would command an Israeli Air Force equipped with French Vautour, Mystère, and Super Mystère aircraft;

The first training flights in Palestine: a glider over the southern coast, June 1939.

The first Israeli fighter planes in 1948.

that he would be the person to buy Mirage fighter jets from France; and that his air force would destroy the Egyptian Air Force on the ground in the first hours of the Six-Day War in 1967.

Other Israeli pilots received their training in semiofficial courses organized by the Haganah under the guise of flying clubs. One of the first courses was in gliding. Young members of the Haganah had already taken up gliding as a sport in the late thirties, so the British could not raise objections. In spite of obstacles by the Mandatory government, the Haganah established in 1940 a small civil airline named Aviron (Hebrew for "airplane"). In garages on kibbutzim and on primitive runways, young Jews took their first lessons in flying.

Now, with the advent of war, the Israelis were extremely fortunate in receiving reinforcement from some highly qualified volunteers. Pilots—the majority from the United

American-made B-17 bombers in the Israeli Air Force prior to a mission, 1948.

Jewish-American volunteer pilots of the 1st Israeli Bomber Squadron, 1948.

Israeli pilots preparing for a mission.

Israeli offensive against Majdal (situated between Tel Aviv and the Gaza Strip and known today as Ashkelon) in 1948.

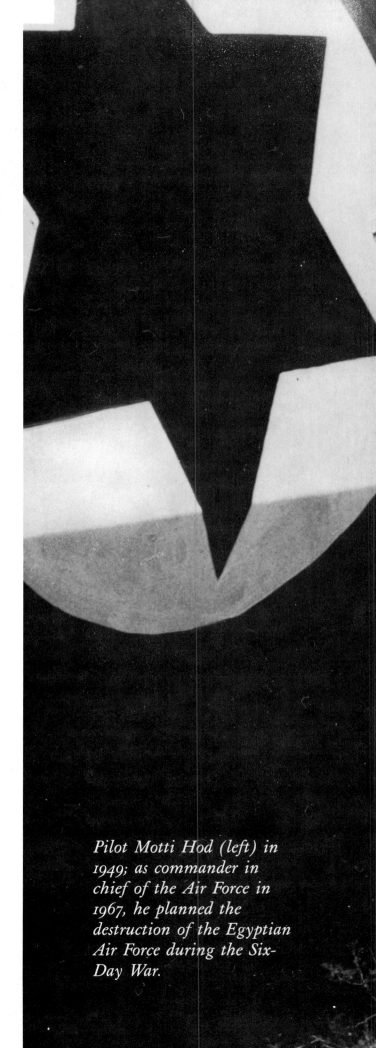

Pilot Motti Hod (left) in 1949; as commander in chief of the Air Force in 1967, he planned the destruction of the Egyptian Air Force during the Six-Day War.

States, others from Britain, South Africa, and France, among other countries—who had acquired their combat experience during World War II, volunteered their assistance in the war effort. Most were Jews, but there were non-Jews among them who decided to come to Palestine because of their identification with the Jewish struggle. Others believed in the Bible and felt that they were helping the People of the Book. In some cases the non-Jews came for the thrill of adventure. It was a remarkable foreign legion of aviators.

The United States imposed a total arms embargo on Israel, ranging from rifles to planes—a ban that would last for some twenty years. In the wake of the 1956 Suez campaign, France became Israel's primary supplier of arms.

However, young American Jews—foremost among them Al Schwimmer, who later established Israel Aircraft Industries—procured cargo planes and bombers in the United States and whisked them across to Europe to be as

close to Israel as possible on the eve of the proclamation of the state.

The Israelis landed cargo planes and three B-17 bombers, smuggled out of the United States, in Czechoslovakia. The first cargo plane, a DC-4 laden with arms, left Czechoslovakia for Eretz Yisrael as early as March 1948. It made a direct flight from Prague to a remote, hastily prepared airstrip. This plane that landed at the improvised airfield under cover of dark brought much-needed heavy machine guns and ammunition.

Within a few days after May 15 it became possible to set up a real airlift between Czechoslovakia and Israel. Efforts were immediately made to fly over to the newborn state the first ten combat aircraft that Israel had purchased, for $200,000 each: Bf 109 Messerschmidts, which the Germans had produced for the Third Reich's Luftwaffe. The Czechs prepared them for shipment, unassembled, along with their spare parts. These were loaded aboard the cargo planes, which arrived in Israel just in time to help stop the advance of Egyptian armored columns that were threatening to break through to the outskirts of Tel Aviv. There was irony in the fact that German-made and -designed combat aircraft, which had sown such terror throughout Europe during World War II, served as the first and most important air shield for the survivors of the Holocaust.

Meantime, however, Egyptian warplanes bombed the Central Bus Station in Tel Aviv in broad daylight, killing and wounding dozens of people.

In the first three weeks following the establishment of the state, the airlift between Czechoslovakia and Israel operated day and night to ferry the Messerschmidts and other weapons. Some planes crashed and their pilots were killed—but the airlift went on unabated.

A direct flight from Czechoslovakia to Israel took eight hours. However, at times the planes (with French permission) had to land in Ajaccio in Corsica; then the flight took fourteen hours. In Yugoslavia also the security forces made a remote airfield available for midflight stopovers from Czechoslovakia. The planes would land in Israel at night, unload their cargo, and immediately turn around back to Czechoslovakia.

There is no doubt that this air shuttle helped Israel hold out against the Arab armies in the first months of the war. In other words, what helped save the day was the cooperation on the part of Communist states, such as Czechoslovakia and Yugoslavia, and planes smuggled out of the United States—which, of all nations, refused to provide military assistance of any sort. Moreover, in August 1948 the U.S. Embassy in Prague intervened, demanding that the Czech Government put a stop to all "illegal" flights of American planes and pilots from its country to Israel. Twenty years would go by before the United States itself would supply the Israeli Air Force with its most advanced fighter-bombers, from the Phantom to the F-15 and F-16. But at the time, in view of the American demand, the Czechs informed Ehud Avriel that the Israeli base in Czechoslovakia would have to be shut down. Before this happened—on July 15—Israeli bombers went out on their first mission, the bombing of Cairo in retaliation for the air raids on Tel Aviv. It is told that King Farouk cowered in his palace that night, when Cairo—never fearing Israeli reprisal and therefore fully illuminated—was bombed from the air at around 10 P.M. By their action the Israelis also repaid the Egyptian King for his troops' shelling of Jerusalem.

The base from which this bombing operation set out was in Czechoslovakia, from where the three B-17 bombers flew over Yugoslavia and Albania on their route to Israel. One of the planes, with a nine-man American-Jewish crew under the command of Captain Ray Kurz and flying at a height of 25,000 feet, crossed into North Africa over the Qattara Depression, dropped its bombs on the Cairo airport, and continued to Israel.

Years later Kurz said, "My ambition had always been to be part of the birth of the State of Israel. That night over Cairo, for the first time in the history of the Jewish people, the Jews gave their enemies a dose of their own medicine—from the air and in great force."

Profile of a Local Hero

BOTH BEFORE and after the drama-packed voyage of the *Exodus,* many legends were spun around the new "Israeli hero." The awe with which world opinion viewed the struggle of the Jewish underground against the British Empire turned to admiration when a handful of Israelis defeated seven regular Arab armies—contrary to the assessments of the world's top military experts.

Israelis too were not sparing in their praise; they expressed, in prose and poetry, admiration for the young men and women who fell on the battlefields of 1948. They were the "silver tray on which the Jewish state was served," as Nathan Alterman, Israel's national poet, described them.

It is Israel's great fortune that this "silver tray" is sufficiently large to have served her in the many wars and operations in which she has been involved—from the Six-Day War in 1967 to the Entebbe operation in 1976; from the smuggling out of missile boats from France in 1969 to the bombing of the Iraqi nuclear reactor in 1981; from the Yom Kippur War in 1973 to the ongoing daily fight against

Palestinian terror and the expulsion of Yasir Arafat and his men from Beirut in 1982.

Initially, these operations frequently elicited applause and sympathy all over the world. Later, these reactions often gave way to anger and fury on the part of many countries. In my opinion, this fury was generated by jealousy of Israel's pluck and daring, and of its decisiveness and operational abilities. As I see it, many of those who leveled criticism did so because Israel went out and did what many states felt that they themselves ought to have done—but were not able to carry out. Israel's ongoing and tenacious fight against terrorism is a good example of this.

A number of important questions arise here: Does the Israeli hero really exist? Is he as macho as he is usually portrayed? Is he an arrogant, overconfident narcissist in love with his macho image? In other words, do the heroes of the *Exodus* really exist in everyday life, and, if so, are they perhaps not enamored with their image to the point of self-destruction? In truth, the Israeli hero is no Japanese Kamikaze.

For over thirty years I have known Israeli

Young tank driver reading prayers prior to an attack.

Members of the Haganah training in the Valley of Jezreel, 1948.

Fighter at the Israeli front, 1948.

fighters in the armored and paratroop corps, the naval commandos, and the air force, Cabinet ministers and members of the Knesset, former and current secret agents; many are among my best friends.

On the strength of this, I can state that in their own country the Israelis have become as "normal" as the people of any other nation. They have their thieves, their whores, and their murderers. Financial, defense, and diplomatic scandals occur in Jerusalem and Tel Aviv, just as they do in any other big city in the world. There are also Israelis who leave their country, disappointed, and move away to

A Haganah fighter in a school of agriculture, 1948.

Member of the Haganah in 1948.

live in other countries, especially the United States.

Along with this, though, Israel also has what most of the nations of the earth do not have: a nucleus of idealists which renews itself with each generation, and which is willing to this day to sacrifice itself in order to ensure the state's existence and security. This nucleus is vital for the existence of the state, which will probably continue to pay a heavy price for its continued existence. There is a price for

the existence of every state—and in the special case of a Jewish state, that price is particularly high.

This is where Israel's secret lies. It has been and continues to be the country's secret weapon even after forty years of statehood. The cemeteries are sad testimony to this. Walking among the tombstones in the military burial plots on Mount Herzl in Jerusalem, at Qiryat Shaul in Tel Aviv, or in Galilee, one sees neatly arranged graves of war heroes

Fighters in the young Israeli Army: members of "Samson's Foxes" commando unit and the "Beasts of the Negev."

*Female members of the Haganah: holding submachine guns and wearing
grenades clipped onto webbing belt.*

of all ages, from different ethnic backgrounds, of different ranks, from lowly privates to generals. Every now and again, you spot the name of a friend.

It is Israel's great fortune that every new generation in the country is at least as good as, if not better than, its predecessors. The kindergartens, schools, and universities of Israel provide increasingly sophisticated young people who have made phenomenal strides in science, medicine, electronics, and engineering. Some of the greatest computer experts in the world are Israelis.

Of course, not all are idealists. Still, it is sufficient that the Israelis raise a few hundred or perhaps a few thousand in each generation to serve as leaders in defending the state in times of crisis.

In the final analysis, it was only a few thousand Israelis who stood firm during the War of Independence and defeated Arab armies supported by many tens of millions. It was a few hundred Israeli fighters who won smashing victories in Jerusalem and the Golan Heights in 1967. During the Yom Kippur War, a few hundred paratroopers and tank corps personnel changed the face of the war when they crossed the Suez Canal.

True, the Israeli Army enlisted hundreds of thousands of men and women in these wars. However, a few hundred set the tone on the battlefield for the remaining thousands of fighters to follow in their footsteps.

Sixteen daring Israeli pilots bombed and destroyed the nuclear reactor near Baghdad in 1981, in an operation of unparalleled complexity. The pilots who, in one amazing air strike, destroyed the Soviet-made surface-to-air missile launchers in the Bekaa Valley in Lebanon in June 1982 acted in the same manner.

And in Damascus, Eli Cohen, the Israeli secret agent on a dangerous mission, living for many years as an Arab, penetrated the Syrian leadership in the early 1960s. He was hanged in the central square of Damascus when, after five years of operations, his true identity was revealed. He left a family in Tel Aviv.

Even though these epic stories have become the subject of many articles, books, and movies, it must be noted that the large majority of Israel's secret operations have not been disclosed and will not be made public for many years to come.

What emerges from all these operations is the profile of the volunteer Israeli fighter: a fighter who has developed since the generation of the *Exodus,* imbued with the same spirit which that odyssey evoked; a fighter educated in the image of those who went to the British gallows singing "Hatikvah"; a level-headed, quiet young man who does not seek prominence and who shuns publicity; a modest man, with a special inner calm, particularly at critical moments; a man possessed of qualities that stem from the very essence of his personality. Every mission, however imaginative it may be, seems perfectly mundane to him the moment he is assigned to perform it. He is always ready to volunteer for missions he knows may cost him his life.

Operation Pirate

FEAR of the impending war with the Arabs led Ben-Gurion to direct not only that every type of weapon and ammunition be procured for the Jews abroad, but also that the supply of arms to the enemy be disrupted and sabotaged. For this, he relied once again on Shaul Avigur, who had run the campaign for illegal immigration to Eretz Yisrael.

In late March 1948 Avigur's men learned that the 450-ton vessel *Lino* had set sail (under the Italian flag) for Syria laden with arms. Initial intelligence reports said the Syrians had purchased in Czechoslovakia 6,000 rifles and 8 million bullets, plus grenades and explosives. The ship reached its first port of call, Molfetta in southern Italy, en route from the Adriatic to the Mediterranean.

Avigur ordered the ship hit at all costs— "on no account must it get into Arab hands" —and put Mounia Mardor in charge of the operation. Mardor had until then been busily engaged in the purchase of arms in Italy and in shipping them secretly to the Haganah in Palestine. Now, however, the *Lino* had to be scuttled, and everyone joined in the effort, including the men of Aliyah Bet.

Mardor and his team initially intended to sink the ship by dropping a bomb from the air. The team included one of the Palmach naval unit's explosive experts, Yossele Dror, a thin, daring, soft-spoken young man, who was stationed in Rome at the time. Twelve years later, Yossele, as he was known, would establish the Israeli Navy's first submarine unit. In those days, however, the Jews did not have a bomb capable of sinking the *Lino,* so Yossele decided to produce a bomb with his own hands that would do the trick, a primitive explosive to be dropped from a private civil airplane flying low over the *Lino.* The first planes purchased by the Jews had just arrived in Italy. These were cargo planes bought from U.S. Army surplus and flown under the guise of a nonexistent Panamanian airline, LAPSA.

While Mardor and Yossele planned their assault on the *Lino,* the vessel set sail for the port of Bari, and the plan had to be altered. Instead of the original bomb, Yossele prepared a mine and persuaded his colleagues to sabo-

217

Loaded with arms for Syria, the Lino *was sunk by the Israelis in the Italian port of Bari.*

tage the *Lino* before it left port. "History will never forgive us," he wrote, "and the blood of our comrades who have given their lives, and those still to fall, will not be atoned if we let this opportunity slip."

Still, there were those who hesitated: Could an operation like this be carried out in Italy? Wouldn't it endanger all Jewish activity in the country, which then served as a base for illegal immigration and the shipment of arms?

But Yossele was adamant. He wanted to get moving and go through with it. He prepared a primitive mine made of a motorcycle tire filled with explosives, to which he attached a delayed-action detonator he had fashioned himself. Under cover of darkness, with a small team, he set out for the *Lino* in a small boat. But the *Lino*'s Italian crew were sitting on deck smoking cigarettes and there was no way to get close to the vessel. Yossele had no option but to send the mine to the bottom of the sea without carrying out his plan.

They approached the ship again the following night in a rubber dinghy. This time they affixed the mine to the ship. They immediately left Bari by car, and only when they got to Rome did they hear the news: The *Lino* had been sunk.* It was April 10, 1947.

Headlines in the Italian newspapers told of the mysterious explosion at the military port of Bari. No one had any idea who had sunk the *Lino*.

The Syrians pressured the Italians to save the cargo from the sunken ship. The Italians retrieved 8,000 rifles—more than the Haganah had thought were on board—and spare parts from the bottom of the harbor and loaded them onto an Italian vessel called the *Argiro,* which was to sail for Alexandria, Egypt.

The Haganah placed two Italian crew members, specially recruited for the operation, aboard the *Argiro* before it sailed from the port of Messina in Sicily. These Italians helped two Israeli agents board the ship on the high seas late one night; the agents presented themselves to the captain as representatives of the Egyptian Government who had come to escort the arms shipment on its voyage. Only later did the two notify the stunned Italian captain that they were in command of the ship and that from that moment on he would have to follow their orders. They instructed him to change course and sail in the direction of Beirut.

This daring operation was code-named "Operation Pirate."

With the aid of radio equipment they had brought aboard with them, the two agents sent a dispatch to their superiors: "The first treasure ship is on its way to Israel."

When news of this reached Tel Aviv, there were those who advised Ben-Gurion that it was unwise to commit acts of piracy at sea and who suggested he hand over the arms to the U.N. They argued that the Arabs were receiving arms freely, whereas Israel was under an embargo, including one imposed by the United States, which had banned shipment of even a rifle to Israel. By handing Arab arms over to the U.N., they contended, Israel would dramatically demonstrate the frustratingly absurd situation in which it found itself.

While this argument raged in Tel Aviv, the *Argiro* was approaching the shores of Eretz Yisrael. Shaul Avigur, though mourning his son, Gur, who had been killed in action, hastened to meet with Ben-Gurion to dissuade him from giving up the arms. Israel was in dire need of these weapons, he argued. In particular, he insisted, every effort should be made to prevent the arms from falling into Arab hands once again—which would probably happen if they were handed over to the United Nations.

With Ben-Gurion's approval, Avigur directed that the navy's two corvettes, Israel's first "battleships," meet the *Argiro* on the high seas. The arms and Italian crew were transferred to the Israeli ships, one of which then rammed the *Argiro* and sank it.

The Arab weapons were then immediately shipped to Israel's various fronts. The Italian crew was housed in an isolated building on Mount Carmel and guarded by plainclothes Israelis, who preserved the crew's anonymity. After seven months, in March 1949, the members of the crew were told they were free to leave. They returned to Italy, where they related how they had transported arms to Egypt,

* There was not a single Italian or other casualty—wounded or killed—as a result of the operation, something that those who carried out the action took pains to mention with great pride in their secret cable of April 10, 1948, sent from Rome to the Haganah HQ in Palestine, saying: "Last night, we sunk the *Lino* in the military port of Bari, together with its entire cargo destined for the Arabs.

"There were no casualties. . . ."

only to find themselves unexpectedly in Israel.†

The Arab press reported that a Syrian major, Fuad Mardam Bey, had transferred the arms to the Jews after being "seduced by a beautiful Czechoslovakian Jewess" and that was the reason "the arms had arrived in Tel Aviv instead of Syria."

Israel maintained silence about the operation for many years. Still, it serves as an excellent illustration of how Israel, from the earliest stages, chose secret warfare both to prevent arms from reaching the Arabs and to obtain arms for itself.

† Once released from detention at Kibbutz Beit Oren on Mount Carmel, where they had been held, the Italian crew were interrogated by the Israeli police and shortly thereafter handed over to the Italian consul in Haifa, and sent back to Italy. This affair was the cause of tension between Rome and the young Israeli Government in Jerusalem, more particularly because the captain of the *Argiro* died from an illness during the time he was held by the Israelis. He took ill in October 1948 and was immediately transferred to a hospital for special treatment. Israeli doctors made every effort to save his life, but he died on December 19, 1948. The cause of his death was certified by Dr. Chaim Sheba, one of Israel's most prominent physicians, as chronic tuberculosis in both lungs from which the captain had been suffering for a considerable time prior to the sea voyage in question. Toward the end of 1949 Jerusalem and Rome, after some harsh exchanges, decided to regard the affair as closed.

The *Altalena*

ONE MONTH after the State of Israel came into being, civil war almost broke out. While the first cease-fire with the Arabs was in force, Jews started firing on Jews. I remember vividly how the news spread around in Tel Aviv: "An Irgun ship is on fire just off the shore of the city, and the Palmach is firing on members of the Irgun."

I rushed to the roof of our three-story building, from which I could see the Tel Aviv shoreline. On this clear June afternoon I saw a black pall of smoke rising out of the blue sea. It was confirmation that the rumors were indeed true. My eyes welled with tears at the thought that Jews were firing on their brethren at a time when there was still a bitter struggle going on against the Arabs.

That evening I listened to a broadcast by Menachem Begin—his last as the commander of the Irgun—over the organization's radio station. To this day I carry the memory of his fury-choked voice: "Jews are shooting Jews," he screamed, telling how they had shelled the ship, on whose deck he had been present: a ship bringing arms to Israeli fighters who were girding themselves for the next round of the War of Independence.

It was one of the most tragic days in the history of Israel. This sad story has different versions and even now is the subject of bitter controversy in Israel. But no one disputes the basic facts.

In the months preceding the establishment of the state, at Begin's request Irgun representatives went abroad to organize shipments of arms and volunteers to prepare for the war against the Arabs. Emissaries of the organization got as far as China and raised $100,000 from the Jewish communities of Shanghai and Tientsin, a huge sum in those days. In the United States, a more substantial group operated openly and raised not only money, but also political support for the Irgun's struggle in Eretz Yisrael.

They bought a landing ship from U.S. Navy surplus and planned to fill it with arms and men and send it to Eretz Yisrael, timed to arrive on the day the British were to leave Palestine. The Irgun rightly considered it a

major contribution to the Jewish forces preparing for the defense of their state.

In France, representatives of the Irgun and the Haganah enjoyed close cooperation with various elements in the government and with French intelligence agencies. For this reason, Port-de-Bouc, on the French Mediterranean coast, was chosen as the base for the ship's departure, and as an arms depot. The French authorities made a gift to the Irgus of a batch of arms.

Ben-Gurion's followers later claimed that French Foreign Minister Georges Bidault had helped the Irgun obtain the arms in retaliation for the troubles the British Government had caused him over the *Exodus.* Begin's supporters insisted Bidault had backed them because, in his eyes, they were like the freedom fighters of the French Resistance against the Nazis in World War II.

As in the case of the *Exodus,* the British Government intervened with the French authorities, and the ship's sailing was delayed until June 11.

The ship was called *Altalena,* an Italian word meaning "seesaw" or "swing"—this had been the pen name of the Irgun's mentor, Zev Jabotinsky.

The ship left the port that day with 780 young men and 169 young women aboard. Heavy arms and ammunition, sufficient to equip an entire brigade, had been loaded into the *Altalena*'s holds. In those days this was a colossal military force. Among other weaponry, the ship carried 5,500 rifles, 300 Bren light machine guns, and 150 heavy machine guns.

As soon as the *Altalena* set sail from Port-de-Bouc, the Irgun high command notified the provisional government in Israel. The Irgun demanded that 20 percent of the weap-

The population of Tel Aviv assembled before the wreck of the Altalena.

The Altalena *in flames, as seen from the city.*

ons be given to its men fighting in Jerusalem. In principle, Ben-Gurion agreed to this. But negotiations between the Irgun and the provisional government were still under way when the *Altalena* arrived offshore, twenty-two miles north of Tel Aviv, and began unloading its weapons. This, too, had been done as agreed with Ben-Gurion.

In the middle of the unloading, however, the Irgun was surprised by volleys of shots fired at them by Israeli soldiers. Begin, who was on the beach, boarded the ship. In the middle of the night it sailed for Tel Aviv. He still believed, as he said much later in many interviews, that there had been a misunderstanding and that everything would be amicably patched up the following morning.

The *Altalena* arrived opposite the Dan Hotel in Tel Aviv and ran aground on a sandbank about a hundred yards from the beach. On this ship were the Jewish volunteers ready to set out for the battlefield, equipped with the arms with which they had already practiced during the voyage. (The immigrants on the *Altalena* afterward did indeed enlist in the Israel Defense Forces, and many of them fell in action against the Arabs.)

But they were not greeted with bouquets.

Instead, Ben-Gurion ordered Palmach units to open fire on the ship, which they did with machine guns. Begin ordered his men not to return fire. Then came the worst blow of all: Shells from a field cannon were fired, hitting the ship, sending the *Altalena* up in flames. Its ammunition stores exploded. Begin stood on the ship's deck and refused to leave until most of its men had jumped overboard. The blue water mixed with the blood of sixteen Jewish immigrants; twenty others were wounded.

The *Altalena* tragedy shocked the public. Ben-Gurion was unequivocal on this issue. He explained to the provisional government why he had ordered that the ship be destroyed: "The transfer of arms by the Irgun threatened the state and laid the ground for a large-scale civil war. . . . A catastrophe was averted by preventing 5,000 rifles and 250 machine guns from falling into the hands of a gang of terrorists. Had this not been prevented, the terrorists would have been capable of murdering both the Jewish state and the freedom of the Jewish population at one and the same time. . . . The government has stated all the time that ships carrying arms must be made over to the government and only to the government. This the members of the Irgun did not want to do. Everyone must ask the simple question: Why didn't they hand over the arms to the government? Since we all have good intentions, we will not judge one another. History will judge each and every one of us for his behavior during these critical times."

If we take into account what the Israelis managed to do on the field of battle against the Arabs with the meager arms they had at their disposal, it is clear that if the weapons on board the *Altalena* had not gone up in flames, they would have provided the young army with significant additional firepower.

But the fact remains that Ben-Gurion was willing to forgo this and possibly even endan-

Aboard the Israel-bound Altalena.

ger the infant state's military situation because he believed there was a greater danger in the continued existence of a "private army"—Begin's organization, "the terrorists," as he called them. Ben-Gurion personally made up with Begin twenty years later—but he never regretted his decision in those dramatic days.

Many months later, Ben-Gurion paid tribute to the cannon that had fired on the *Altalena* and called it "the holy cannon." He and his followers for years claimed that Begin's intention was to use the weapons from the *Altalena* to conduct a putsch and seize the legal power of government from Ben-Gurion. Most of the citizens of the State of Israel for many years believed this version, which helped Ben-Gurion brand Begin with the stigma of being a "fascist," relegating him to parliamentary opposition for thirty years.

To this day not one document or any other scrap of evidence has been revealed to substantiate Ben-Gurion's accusation. Indeed, when Begin became Prime Minister in 1977 he acted in the most democratic and legalistic manner, even in the eyes of his most bitter adversaries. On the other hand, during Ben-Gurion's great years as Prime Minister he became known as a leader who rejected any attempt to disagree with his decisions.

The *Altalena* tragedy in the midst of the War of Independence is indicative of the fact that the fraternal hatred between Israelis was no less dangerous than that which had led to the destruction of the Second Temple during the days of the Roman siege of Jerusalem, as described by the great Jewish historian Flavius Josephus in his book *The History of the Jewish War*. This hatred, which has flared up again among the Jews regarding the controversy over Jewish settlements in Judea and Samaria, is the greatest danger to Israel in the coming years.

Menachem Begin in Tel Aviv, 1948.

Menachem Begin inspecting a brigade of the Irgun.

David Ben-Gurion with some of his officers.

On the first Saturday after the *Altalena* catastrophe, I rushed down to the Tel Aviv shore. With other youngsters, I swam to the charred hull of the ship. The smell of fire and explosives still hung in the air. We dived down into the water near the ship and brought up charred rifles from the seabed. We played with them, but our hearts were heavy.

Ben-Gurion's defenders in the *Altalena* affair claim to this day that it was a "historic decision" by the first Prime Minister. By shelling the *Altalena* he gave a clear sign that he would no longer countenance the existence of private armies in Eretz Yisrael.

A few months later, even before the War of Independence ended, Ben-Gurion ordered the disbanding of the Palmach—without a shot being fired, but on the very same grounds. Just as he feared Begin's "private army" on the right, so he feared a private army on the left, since the Palmach was identified in part with the extreme left wing of the political spectrum. And by dismantling the "private armies," Ben-Gurion also clipped the wings and dissipated the power of his potential opponents for the right to govern the State of Israel for many years to come.

Between Jerusalem and Washington

FROM Israel's first moments as a nation, the United States lent critical support. President Harry Truman was personally involved for many months in the key decisions relating to the Palestinian question, beginning with American support for the Partition Plan. Jewish leaders in the United States found an attentive ear in the White House when they came to request support for the young state. Truman received ongoing reports about the battle between the Jews and Arabs, including secret CIA analyses that followed the developments of the battles in Palestine.

On July 8, 1948, CIA Director Roscoe H. Hillenkoetter sent Truman a secret memorandum, in which he said:

"Since 15 May 1948, when the UK abandoned its mandate over Palestine, the Arabs and Jews have experienced four weeks of bitter hostilities and four weeks of uneasy truce.

"Neither war nor peace, however, has in any way weakened the determination of the Jews to establish a sovereign state of Israel or the determination of the Arabs to prevent the establishment of such a state. The period of hostilities led to a military stalemate; the truce has favored the Jews. . . .

"In the resumption of full-scale hostilities, the Jewish forces will probably attempt to consolidate their positions in the coastal area and Galilee and to gain control over Jerusalem. The Arabs will probably try to break the military stalemate which had developed prior to the truce. They will attempt to reimpose their blockade of Jerusalem by cutting the Tel Aviv supply route and will try to isolate Tel Aviv from the hinterland by making concerted advances with the Egyptians, Transjordan, and Iraqi armies. The Syria Army will probably launch a limited offensive in northeastern Galilee.

"The success of the Arab campaign is doubtful in view of acute ammunition shortages. Unless the Arabs can force political concessions from Israel within the next two months, they will probably be compelled by logistic difficulties to withdraw most of their army units from Palestine. However, they can be expected to support guerilla activities indefinitely. Arab guerilla incursions, political non-recognition, and economic sanctions will completely isolate Israel from the rest of the Near East. Under such circumstances, its security will be continuously threatened, its economy stifled, and its future existence consequently will be entirely dependent on the continuing good will of some outside power or powers."

Forty years later, it remains one of the more amazingly accurate predictions ever made about the Middle East.

The battle between the Jews and Arabs interested the CIA on a number of levels, particularly regarding how it would influence the position of the U.S.S.R. in the Middle East. The United States was concerned at the time with the expansionist plans of Soviet communism under the leadership of Joseph Stalin. Washington was worried that the vacuum created by the disintegration of the British Empire's foothold in the Middle East might be filled by the Soviet Union.

Washington was also concerned about the future of its increasingly close relations with the Arab oil states. But there were many in the U.S. administration who supported the young State of Israel for moral and political reasons. The American sense of justice, and the shock felt over the disclosure of the Nazi mass exterminations, led them to support the newborn state. There were, nevertheless, many in the administration who were hesitant to go too far in support of Israel.

On July 27, 1948, the CIA sent a more detailed report to the Secretary of Defense. According to a note in the report, "The intelligence organizations of the departments of State, Army, Navy and the Air Force have concurred in this report." At the time, a UN-inspired cease-fire was officially in force in Eretz Yisrael. The CIA report noted that "the present intentions of the USSR are to promote instability and insecurity throughout the Middle East and to undermine the positions of the

US and the UK therein. To do so, the USSR has given, and presumably will continue to give, support in varying degrees to both Israel and the Arab countries. . . ." In regard to the position of the Arab states in the war, the CIA report stated:

"The Arab people were confident of victory and were assured by their leaders that the truce would not be extended. Their bitterness may well erupt into violence against their governments or the Western powers or both. If their wrath is turned against their leaders, some of the Arab governments, in an attempt to survive, may well resume the Palestine war. Arab leaders, however, will first make every effort to turn the anger of their people against the UN, the US, and the UK, or even against one another.

"The timing of such developments cannot be predicted because they depend partly on spontaneous eruptions of popular feelings, which are subject to violent change, and partly on organized agitation. Rioting, however, has already developed in Cairo. Serious Jewish violations of the truce (particularly the bombing of Arab cities) would further inflame Arab governments to discontinue the truce. Communist agents in the Arab countries will probably exert themselves to stir up the people against their government in order to bring about the downfall of the present regime as well as to destroy the truce . . .

"The Jews, with a de facto government and because of their military strength and the political support of the US and the USSR, are in an extremely strong position. . . . The Arabs, in spite of their weakness, have given no official indications that they are prepared to recognize Israel as defined in the UN partition plan. At the present time no Arab government feels it could survive if it consented to negotiate with Israeli representatives. . . ."

In referring to the military situation at the end of July 1948, the CIA report emphasized with great precision that "the Jews gained considerably from a military point of view. They strengthened and improved their existing fortifications and built new ones in the areas recently taken over from the Arabs. They improved the by-pass road to Jerusalem, which skirts Arab-held Latrun and Bab el Wad on the main road from Jerusalem to Tel Aviv. They recruited and trained troops both aboard and in Palestine; and reinforcements were flown in from abroad. They increased their supply of tanks, airplanes, and artillery. The Jews brought heavy artillery into the Jerusalem area, and are reported to have acquired at least 13 German ME-109 fighter planes—which can be converted into light bombers—and 3 B-17s. (They are now reported to possess a total of 60 ME-109s, of which 24 are operational.) The food situation in Jerusalem was greatly improved during the truce.

"The Arabs made certain gains during the truce, but these were insignificant compared to the Jewish gains. The Arabs received some Italian and Belgian arms, and brought more arms and ammunition to the front.

"The truce resulted in so great an improvement in the Jewish capabilities that the Jews may now be strong enough to launch a full-scale offensive and drive the Arab forces out of Palestine. Events during the truce, and the enormous increase in Jewish strength resulting from them considerably change the previously held estimate of the probable course of the war in Palestine. The Arabs' logistical position generally is very bad and their ammunition supply is exceedingly low. It is estimated that they could not continue to fight, even on the previous moderate scale, for more than two to three months."

In the same report in July 1948, the CIA also analyzed Soviet political objectives in the Middle East, which have not changed to this day, with great precision: "a) The ultimate objective of Soviet policy vis-à-vis the Middle East is the assumption of the dominant role in the area. b) To implement this main objective, Soviet policy is directed towards the accomplishment of four secondary objectives; (1) Instability in the Arab World. (2) A complete break between the US and the Arab states. (3) Strained relations between the US and the UK concerning Middle East policy. (4) A complete break between the UK and the Arab states.

". . . With the above objectives in mind the USSR voted for the UN partition of Palestine. From November 1947 to May 1948, it consistently supported partition, but took no initiative in urging effective action to implement partition. Officially the Soviet position was unimpeachable; unofficially, the Kremlin was content to sit back and watch matters go from bad to worse in Palestine. The Soviet delegation loudly denounced and obstructed the US proposal for a temporary trusteeship over Palestine, the one possibility which might have prevented an Arab-Jewish war after 15 May. Since 15 May the delegation has been lukewarm on truce attempts and has obstructed mediation efforts. On 7 July it abstained in the Security Council from voting for the resolution to extend the four weeks' truce. Although it voted for the resolution on 15 July ordering the belligerents to cease hostilities, it abstained from voting on the proposal to give the UN Mediator authority to negotiate a settlement between Jews and Arabs.

". . . The future policy of the USSR vis-à-vis Palestine will aim at consolidating the objectives already partially attained. It will continue to be the Soviet plan to follow a line of opportunism and readiness to exploit what the USSR considers US and UK mistakes. While continuing to support the partition scheme, the USSR may be expected to abstain on or to block any UN action which is likely to bring Jewish-Arab hostilities to a permanent end.

231

"In such an event, it may be expected that the USSR will shift the emphasis of its propaganda from 'Jewish Independence' to 'US Imperialism in Israel' and under the latter slogan will woo the Arab governments with promises of military advisers and supplies. It can be expected to 'encourage' its own candidates in the political turmoil which will follow Arab Military defeats. By such methods it will continue its drive toward the attainment of its basic objective, the assumption of the dominant role in the Middle East."

In other words, as far back as 1948, the CIA and the U.S. administration in general were able to make a precise evaluation of how the Soviet Union would act in the Middle East in getting the greatest mileage for itself out of the establishment of the State of Israel.

The Arabists in the Pentagon and State Department tried to use this to block Truman's support of Israel. From time to time they succeeded. Thus, for example, an American arms embargo was imposed on Israel, which lasted about twenty years, as a result of which Israel turned to France to purchase weapons and planes.

Ben-Gurion himself understood the Soviet approach from the start. He decided, above all, that Israel would adopt a pro-American orientation in its foreign affairs.

The basic American policy during those years of embargo was, however, very friendly and included political, moral, and financial support. Only many years later, when the Soviet Union had become the arms supplier of Israel's archenemies, and the Israelis had annihilated advanced Soviet weapons on the battlefield, did Israel become America's military ally, helping the United States more than any other country to contain Soviet expansion in the Middle East.

A Galilee Without Peace

THE ISRAELI forces' conquest of Nazareth on July 16, 1948, represented a turning point in the Israeli offensive aimed at liberating the whole of Galilee and incorporating it into the State of Israel. The surrender of Nazareth led to the collapse of the entire Arab forces in Lower Galilee.

Credit for this offensive must be given to another outstanding commander in Israel's War of Independence, General Moshe Carmel, who later served as a government minister for many years. Ben-Gurion knew how important Nazareth was to the Christian world; thus he sent Carmel an urgent message on the eve of the city's conquest: "If Nazareth is about to fall, you must set up a special force in advance, one that is both loyal and well disciplined, and one that will not allow a single other Jewish soldier to set foot in Nazareth and will not allow any looting or desecration of monasteries and churches."

When Ben-Gurion later visited Carmel at the command headquarters he had established in Nazareth, he saw for himself that his orders had been carried out to the letter. Nothing in the Christian holy places had been damaged. He wrote in his diary: "I traveled around the city of Nazareth. It has been a good few years since I was last there. Our relations with the local inhabitants are good. Only the Christian monks there are involved in fighting among themselves, and they tattle on each other to the government."

The Israeli settlements and kibbutzim in Galilee withstood months of siege and bloody battles, both before and after May 15. Jews suffered heavy casualties, including those who fell in unsuccessful operations, but Israel eventually conquered Acre and liberated the coastal strip of western Galilee.

It almost seemed as though the British were intent on presenting Galilee to the Arabs on a silver platter. As early as the end of April, even before the establishment of the state, they handed over their fortified police stations, set on strategic high points, to the Arabs.

Safed, a city holy to the Jews, was conquered after bitter battles in the hilly regions.

233

In the course of this campaign, Yigal Allon and his men played a key role. The Jewish minority of 1,500 held out for many long months, despite facing 10,000 Arab residents, the bulk of whom fled in panic. Earlier, the Israelis had gained control of Tiberias on the shores of the Sea of Galilee.

These successes were particularly impressive in light of the fact that regular army units from Syria and Lebanon had come to the assistance of the Arab partisan forces fighting against Jewish settlements in Galilee.

After May 15 Israel faced four adversaries in the northern front: the Syrians in the east, the Iraqis in the south, the Lebanese in the north, and Kaukji's Arab Redemption Army in the heart of Galilee.

These armies were equipped with modern cannonry and armor, while the Israelis had virtually no artillery at all. In liberating Safed, the Israelis used a "Davidka"—a homemade mortar that caused more noise than damage. When two French-made 65-mm cannon arrived, they were sent directly to the Jordan Valley to stop a Syrian armored attack on kibbutzim there. These cannon were so outdated that they immediately earned the nickname "Napoleonchik."

In the end, after the Syrians had destroyed the kibbutzim of Shaar Hagolan and Massada, they were stopped by a Molotov cocktail at the gates of Kibbutz Degania. The Syrian forces withdrew. The burned-out tank to this day stands in this thriving kibbutz, a reminder of those bitter days and testimony to the exceptional fighting spirit the Israelis evidenced in their War of Independence. The Arab Redemption Army under the command of Fawzi al-Kaukji outdid them all in its activity in the Galilee. It numbered two thousand fighters, volunteers from all the Arab states, and was equipped with cannon-mounted armored cars and 75-mm cannon. Kaukji's men had been equipped and trained by, and was subordinate to, the supreme command in Damascus. This army attacked kibbutzim, blocked roads in preparation for the overall Arab invasion, hit settlements, and inflicted large losses on the Jews. After the invasion, it fought in the heart of Galilee, attacking and bombarding Jewish settlements. From time to time, regular Syrian units came to the assistance of the Redemption Army. The Golan Heights was in Syrian hands, leaving all the settlements in the Jordan Valley and Upper Galilee within range of their artillery.

It was only three months after the conquest of Nazareth that Moshe Carmel delivered a death blow to Kaukji's five regiments. In battles lasting four days (October 28–31), the Israelis chased the remnants of the Redemption Army from Galilee. One of its units surrendered with all equipment and weapons intact, and a Syrian unit that tried to come to its aid was wiped out. Kaukji himself escaped to Lebanon, together with tens of thousands of panic-stricken Arab villagers who abandoned their homes when they saw their defender run for his life.

Moshe Carmel described Kaukji in a book he wrote after the war: "Kaukji's modes of operation were very strange in our eyes. This adventurer, despite his great defeats, despite the complete annihilation of his forces, and even in the face of our growing strength, never gave up his dreams of coming back and conquering Galilee . . . He continued to dream of great and wondrous victories, and to inspire his army with baseless fantasies."

This is an appropriate description for most of the Arab kings, presidents, and commanders who sent their men to die on the battlefields of Eretz Yisrael for a hate-inspired illusion.

Ben-Gurion's feelings of triumph were never free of his anxious concern for the future. With amazing realism he foresaw the future well before the war was over, even though he was convinced of ultimate victory. He wrote in his diary: "An end to the war?

Will there be an end, even if the war ends now? And if a peace is signed, has there ever been a war that wasn't preceded by a peace? One has to view not only decisions and documents, but also the realities of history. What is our reality? The Arab people were defeated by us. Will they forget this quickly? Seven hundred thousand overwhelmed thirty million. Will they forget this insult? It must be assumed that Arabs have a sense of pride. We will make every effort to achieve peace, but peace requires two sides. Is there any assurance that they will not seek to avenge themselves against us? We must face truth: we won not because our army wrought miracles, but because the Arab army is rotten. Will this rot continue forever?"

Like all the great leaders of his time, including De Gaulle, Churchill, and Gandhi, Ben-Gurion lived with a sense of anxiety for the future of his people, even in moments of great achievement and victory—and perhaps especially because of such feats. The American press simplistically termed him a "pistol-packing prophet," he would have preferred a hoe. "We must think of the means," he wrote, "to maintain our fighting capabilities together with our ability to build and develop."

Twenty-two years later, Ben-Gurion was still concerned over the continuing wars between Israel and the Arab states. He expressed this feeling in his study on Keren Keyemet Boulevard in Tel Aviv, in an interview with the eminent French author, Joseph Kessel, a member of the French Academy.

I sat in on that conversation in the spring of 1970 and studied the two of them with curiosity and interest. It was a meeting between a lion of literature and the lion of the State of Israel. Between two Jews, from different countries, exceptional in each of their own fields but united in their concern for the fate of the Jewish people and the future of Israel. At the time Joseph Kessel had returned to Israel to get a closer view of its heroic fight against the Egyptians along the Suez Canal during the War of Attrition. Almost every day Israelis were killed and wounded along the Canal. I followed the conversation between these two great men. They both showed signs of their age, but their faces were as full of power and expression as ever. Two unique men sitting opposite one another, each curiously eyeing the other: Ben-Gurion with his peculiar white-haired crown, and Kessel with his gray-white mound of hair. Living personalities from Jewish and world history.

Ben-Gurion told Kessel that peace depended on the Israelis' belief in the justice of their cause, Faith is the ultimate source for the spirit: "Because the Israelis possess such spirit, they will one day achieve the greatest of all victories—peace with their neighbors."

The Generals
of Israel

THE War of Independence was to witness the emergence of four young military leaders who, over the next forty years, played critical roles in ensuring the defense of the Jewish state. Moshe Dayan and Yigal Allon, the most remarkable of all the 1948 war heroes, were then already known. Dayan, easily recognizable by the black patch over his left eye, was particularly famous. But it is generally agreed that Allon was the most brilliant leader of the War of Independence.

Younger and less well known for their exploits in Israel's first war were Yitzhak Rabin and Ariel Sharon. The latter, a twenty-year-old sublieutenant at the outbreak of the war, was seriously wounded near Latrun, just ten days after the Arab invasion of the new state.

All four had one thing in common: they were all born in Eretz Yisrael. They are the embodiment of the Sabra, the native-born Israeli named for the fruit of the Barbary fig tree—tough and prickly on the outside, tender and sweet on the inside. Dayan, Allon, and Sharon were all born in rural communi-

Commander Moshe Dayan in 1948.

ties; Rabin, although born in Jerusalem, received a secondary education at the Agricultural School of Kadouri on Mount Tabor.

These details are important to understanding the four generals; brought up to be farmers, they shared a link with the land of Eretz Yisrael. Manual labor, especially farm labor, was an essential ingredient of the new Jewish personality being formed in Israel.

It was Yigal Allon who best explained the link between the new Jew and his land: "At the foot of Mount Tabor, there is a village called Kfar Tabor where the peasants honor the land. I was born there in October 1918. I felt a great love for the smells of my native village: the smell of the almond trees and wildflowers, and, above all, the smell of the earth after the first rains. For me, the smell of hay evokes the smell of love."

Through this intense involvement with the land, the four generals learned firsthand the need for a strategic defense of Eretz Yisrael. Born with an intense attachment to the soil of their homeland, they developed a belief in their right to the land, a belief more strongly held than that of those who claimed Eretz Yisrael in the name of biblical history.

As chief of staff and then Defense Minister on the eve of the Six-Day War, Dayan would play a critical role in shaping the most glori-

238

ous moment of Israel's military history. Later, as Foreign Minister under Menachem Begin, he contributed to the Camp David process that led to a peace treaty with Egypt.

Allon was to serve several governments of Israel in such posts as Foreign Affairs Minister and Vice Prime Minister. Rabin served with Dayan as chief of staff in 1967; later, as Prime Minister, he made the difficult decision to launch the miraculous mission to rescue the hostages at Entebbe Airport in Uganda. Today he is Minister of Defense.

Sharon, even more so than his colleagues, would distinguish himself on the field in later wars, winning decisive battles against the Egyptians in 1956, 1967, and 1973. In 1982, as Defense Minister, he led the Israeli attack against the PLO stranglehold on Lebanon. Accused by *Time* magazine of responsibility for the massacre of Palestinians at the Sabra and Shatilla camps in Lebanon, he proved the accusation false, clearing his name in a dramatic libel trial in New York that made both international headlines and legal history.

Following 1948, I came to know very closely the new young leaders of Israel, particularly these four generals. As a member of the first generation of the Jewish state, I was very strongly influenced by them, and was impressed by their exceptional bravery on the battlefield, their intelligence, their imagination, and their ability to make crucial decisions under heavy pressure.

I watched their transformation from military leadership to political leadership. Like their mentor, Ben-Gurion, they stressed the importance of the Israeli spirit, which—more than tanks and planes—they knew would encourage the settling of the land.

Dayan and Allon met for the first time in the late 1930s, when the Haganah began organizing special units to defend the Yishuv. They worked directly under Yitzhak Sadeh, founder of the Palmach. One of the most famous photos in the history of the young state

Yitzhak Rabin and Yigal Allon.

shows Sadeh, wearing khaki shorts, holding his two young protégés by the shoulders, as if they were his proud sons.

From the start, Dayan and Allon were considered the rising stars of the underground. They possessed personal charm, but more importantly their natural leadership ability became evident at a young age.

Ezer Weizman.

Yitzhak Rabin (center) a high-ranking officer in the Palmach, 1948.

While taking part in a raid against Vichy French forces in Syria in June 1941, Dayan was wounded, causing the loss of his eye. For the next forty years, until his death, the heroism and imagination of the State of Israel would be symbolized in the black eyepatch he constantly wore.

In the Soviet Union, young Jews, their Zionist pride first awakened by Israel's smashing victory in 1967, secretly greeted each other with a simple signal: a hand held over their left eye.

Allon, as the Haganah's chief strategist, was to distinguish himself even more than Dayan in the War of Independence. As the Palmach's twenty-nine-year-old commanding general, it was he who first developed and applied the strategic military doctrine of Israel: indirect attack, surprise assaults against unsuspected areas behind enemy lines.

The young officers who rose from the ranks during the War of Independence became firmly convinced that Israel could never afford to lose a war, a conviction born of a people who realize that they have their backs to the sea. The motto born of that war—"No choice"—remains apt today. Israel has no choice but to constantly win, to achieve the impossible.

It is in this way that Israeli generals differ from their colleagues in other countries, a difference best expressed by Sharon, who has been compared to George Patton and Douglas MacArthur:

"An Israeli general cannot afford to lose a single war. Generals in other countries can lose a battle or a war—rarely are other countries' existences threatened if they are conquered. In Israel, to lose a war would mean more than losing independence—it would mean losing the state.

"Second, the Israeli general must participate in national efforts, not only in times of war but in times of peace as well. He must contribute to the building of the state when the war is over. That is why the Army takes part in projects that have nothing to do with defense, such as absorbing immigrants or building new settlements."

Thus both Dayan and Sharon would serve as Ministers of Agriculture, Allon as Minister of Absorption and, later, Education and Foreign Affairs.

It's as if the author of the script of Israeli history had assigned the same limited cast repeating permanent roles in the ongoing drama. Yet these heroes have continually distinguished themselves in each of their undertakings and every crisis, a performance born of the life-and-death struggle of 1948.

In 1956 Prime Minister Ben-Gurion and Chief of Staff Dayan masterminded Israel's conquest of the entire Sinai Peninsula in just one hundred hours, a victory highlighted by the parachuting near the Suez Canal of Israeli troops commanded by Colonel Ariel Sharon.

In 1967 Defense Minister Dayan and Chief of Staff Rabin oversaw the tremendous conquests of the Six-Day War as part of a government that included Vice Premier Allon and an army in which General Sharon's armored division broke through Egyptian strongholds to open up the road to the Suez Canal.

In 1973 Defense Minister Dayan was shaken by the surprise Egyptian attack on Yom Kippur afternoon. "It's the destruction of the Third Temple," a depressed Dayan told

Yigal Allon, the brilliant commander of the Palmach.

Prime Minister Golda Meir. But thanks to Reserve General Sharon, an Israeli defeat turned into a victory when his troops crossed the Suez Canal into Egypt and surrounded Cairo's Third Army.

I remember well the days following that action; as Egyptian artillery bombarded us, Dayan visited the front, asking Sharon to show him from as close a point as possible the Israeli beachheads in Egypt. I watched the two of them—Dayan, the old battle horse, and Sharon at his side. I could feel their determination to beat the Egyptians.

Suddenly Egyptian jet fighters, MiGs and Soukhois, appeared in the sky, releasing bombs along our convoy. The ground shook under the bombardment. I quickly took off my helmet and handed it to Dayan; I was more concerned for the safety of this worldwide symbol of Israeli courage than for myself. But he refused my offer with a smile, saying, "In this war, every man takes care of himself."

In 1977 Sharon worked closely at the side of Menachem Begin, Israel's greatest Prime Minister after Ben-Gurion. The agonies of 1973 were rewarded in the process that led to a peace treaty with Egypt.

As he stepped off the plane in Ben-Gurion Airport on that historic Saturday night in November 1977, Anwar al-Sadat asked Begin a question that would be quoted in every radio and newspaper story: "Is General Sharon here?"

There is a direct relationship between each of Israel's victories in the Sinai and the signing of the peace with Egypt. Sadat has reminded the Israelis of an important historical lesson, one that is not always understood: only when they realize that they cannot defeat Israel on the battlefield will the Arabs agree to make peace.

I witnessed the expression of this lesson on May 21, 1981, when I accompanied Ariel Sharon on a visit with Sadat in Egypt. The Egyptian President received him in the enormous room, decorated with Persian carpets, reserved for important dignitaries.

For a long time, the two men sat in their Louis XVI armchairs, looking into each other's eyes. It was a true peace without words—peace between strong men.

Murder in Jerusalem

ON FRIDAY afternoon, September 17, 1948, a convoy of U.N. cars traveling through Jerusalem suddenly found its way blocked. Three men, armed with automatic weapons, jumped from a jeep and started firing. Then one assailant ran over to the vehicles and shot the occupants of one car. Count Folke Bernadotte and his French assistant, Colonel André Serreau, had been assassinated.

Ben-Gurion, who soon received a report about the murder from Moshe Dayan, newly appointed commander of the Jerusalem region, was utterly shocked. He immediately gave orders that every effort be made to find the murderers without delay. The prime suspect was the Stern Group.

Folke Bernadotte had been appointed by the United Nations as a special mediator for the Palestine problem. When it became apparent to the U.N. in June 1948 that the Arab-Israeli War had in fact nullified the Partition Plan, the international forum tried to intervene in the course of events. The Arabs, with British support, took advantage of the U.N.

for their purposes. Each time the Arabs felt the Israelis were achieving success in the field, the U.N. imposed a cease-fire. The United States and France naturally gave their support to these cease-fires.

Actually, both sides utilized the cease-fires to prepare their forces for future offensives. In the final analysis, the Israelis succeeded in exploiting these breaks far more effectively than the Arabs. After every cease-fire the Israelis launched successful offensives, thereby gaining control of Galilee and strengthening their hold on Jerusalem.

On August 2, 1948, the Israeli Government decided to appoint a "military governor" for the new city of Jerusalem, effectively annexing it as part of the State of Israel. Moshe Dayan, was appointed commander of Jerusalem, replacing David Shaltiel. The Egyptian Army had not yet been thrown out of the south, and the expanses of the Negev were not yet in Israeli hands.

At this point Bernadotte came forward with a proposal to stop the war—a proposal that, naturally, gained the support of the U.N.

Moshe Dayan in Jerusalem in September 1948, at the time of the assassination of Count Bernadotte.

and most of the superpowers. His conditions were that the Galilee become part of the Jewish state, while the Negev—contrary to the Partition Plan—be given to the Arabs, who sought territorial continuity between Jordan and Egypt. Britain considered the Negev an important area for future strategic air bases to serve the Empire, which still controlled the Middle East. But the main part of the Bernardotte plan was that the Jews would be granted "municipal autonomy" over a small part of Jerusalem, while the city as a whole would be internationalized in strict accordance with the Partition Plan. Bernadotte wanted to impose this settlement in time for the upcoming meeting of the General Assembly in Paris, at the Chaillot Palace. The day after he arrived on a visit to Jerusalem, the mediator was assassinated.

It is clear today that the Stern Group committed this act in the belief that Bernadotte, with the support of the superpowers, would have imposed his plan on the young state. They feared that the Negev, representing two thirds of Israel's territory, might be detached from it. The Israeli authorities, however, never succeeded in identifying the assailants or bringing them to justice.

The newly established Israeli secret service, however, and particularly one of its commanders, Isser Harel, were convinced that the assassins came from the ranks of the Stern Group. This was the same Isser Harel who would later build the Mosad, the Institute for Security and Intelligence—an agency whose exploits would become feared and respected throughout the world.

Ben-Gurion decided that this was an opportune time to disband the Stern Group, just as he had earlier dismantled Begin's Irgun in the wake of the *Altalena* affair. He ordered Moshe Dayan to arrest all Stern Group members in Jerusalem, except for those who were already serving in units of the IDF. "You must act swiftly and without mercy," he ordered Dayan, adding that extra units be moved to Jerusalem for this purpose, even though they were needed on other fronts. Ben-Gurion had no faith in the police.

Ben-Gurion also took advantage of the uproar over the assassination to order the breakup of Irgun units in Jerusalem, where they were still operating independently, even after the *Altalena* affair.

On the day following the murder, sixty Jews were rounded up and hundreds of weapons confiscated. Ben-Gurion was particularly interested in finding the Sternist leaders, among them Yitzhak Shamir. As a "dangerous terrorist," Shamir was on the "most wanted" list.

Ben-Gurion thus not only made it clear that he would no longer tolerate the existence of private armies, but that he had also gained the upper hand over Begin and Shamir, his former rivals in the struggle against the British. So Shamir secretly met with Shaul Avigur and promised him that the Stern Group would never set up a Jewish underground directed against the government of Israel. Only then did Ben-Gurion agree to pardon all Stern Group detainees; years later Isser Harel would appoint Shamir to the post of senior operations officer in the Mosad, where he was to do to Arab enemies what he had done so effectively in the underground against the British. This was undoubtedly an important stage toward the "legitimizing" of Shamir, who became Prime Minister in September 1983.

To this very day, however, most of the nations of the world still do not recognize Jerusalem as the capital of Israel and instead maintain their embassies in Tel Aviv.

Israel in the Sinai Desert

AT THE END of December 1948, the Israeli Army achieved its greatest success in its first war against Egypt. Israeli units entered the Sinai Desert and captured Abu Ageila, a key strategic point, and advanced on the capital of the northern Sinai—the town of Al-Arish and its airport. Just six months after having reached within thirty kilometers of Tel Aviv, the Egyptian Army was on the brink of a shattering defeat. But there were still huge British military encampments along the Suez Canal—and King Farouk had the support of the British Government. London made overtures to Washington to apply pressure on Ben-Gurion to withdraw from the Sinai.

Israeli convoy during the battle for the Negev, 1948.

246

Israeli cavalry in 1948.

Israeli infantry offensive in the Negev, 1948.

This Sinai campaign was conducted by the commander of the Southern Front, Yigal Allon. Throughout the War of Independence, Allon stood out as a brilliant general in the new army. Each time his units went on the offensive, he sought to beat the enemy by indirect approach, flanking the enemy or coming from its rear avoiding bloody frontal attacks wherever possible so as to keep casualties to a minimum.

Allon, a fine-looking man and a young general, was a favorite not only with women but with the soldiers who fought under him. He had great personal charm, and his approach to people was a direct one, open to his subordinates.

As commander of the Palmach during the War of Independence, he fought in all the crucial sectors. His men had blunted the Syrians and Lebanese in Galilee, where they lost some of their finest fighters. They had taken part in decisive battles in the Jerusalem hills and in the city itself. Only after victories in

248

An entrenched Israeli position.

Hagolan and Massada in the Jordan Valley. In the Negev there were also kibbutzim that fell to the Egyptian and, when later recaptured, were found to have been totally destroyed. But it was the ability of the kibbutzim to hold out as long as they did, which made it possible for the units of the Israeli Army to organize themselves for an effective offensive. It is for this reason that even now, Israel's defense deployment is also based on Jewish settlement along its border.

In the south, beginning on May 15, Egyptian tanks, artillery, and mortars destroyed one kibbutz after another. Sometimes the kibbutzim were bombed by planes as well. Members of the kibbutzim—men as well as women—fought from trenches and bunkers amid their ruined houses, using light arms. That was the situation at Nirim, Negba and Kfar Darom, as well as at Yad Mordechai and other places. Most of the kibbutzim had only a handful of men—but these brave people generally managed to prevent the Egyptian soldiers from capturing the battered kibbutzim.

The kibbutzim in the Negev had for many months been under a tough siege, and it was difficult—and sometimes impossible—to have supplies delivered to them. The Palmach's Negev brigade became part of the defense deployment with a view to going on to a counteroffensive. The Egyptians, meanwhile, had advanced to Majdal and Isdud (known today as the flourishing Jewish towns of Ashkelon and Ashdod) in the direction of Tel Aviv. There they were halted by the Givati Infantry Brigade,* which with its slogan "death to the invaders" was involved in hand-to-hand fighting with the Egyptians. The number of Israeli dead and wounded against the Egyptians ran into thousands.

these areas did the Israelis turn their attention to expelling the Egyptians from Eretz Yisrael.

The campaign against the Egyptian Army was a prolonged and very bloody one. Originally it had been the kibbutzim in the south and in the Negev that had stopped the Egyptian brigades, just as in the Jordan Valley and in Galilee kibbutzim had halted the Syrian and Lebanese armies. Other kibbutzim had withstood the might of the Iraqi Army and other Arab forces. The Haganah concept of defense, in which settlements were established for purposes of containing attacks by Arab regulars until Jewish military reinforcements could arrive, proved itself in the War of Independence, even when it came to holding out against tanks and artillery. The Gush Etzion kibbutzim had fallen, as had those of Shaar

* The Givati Infantry Brigade was named after its founder and courageous commander during the War of Independence, Shimon Avidan, whose code name in the Palmach had been "Givati." In setting up the brigade, Avidan recruited Haganah members from the Tel Aviv and Southern Region.

Egyptian surrender in the Negev, early 1949.

For the most part, the Israelis had no tanks to throw into battle against the Egyptian armored corps. So they devised a motto that has remained part and parcel of Israeli military thinking to this very day: "It is not the tank that will win, but the man." The Givati Brigade set up a commando unit mounted on jeeps, which was nicknamed "Samson's Foxes," and it carried out numerous attacks on Egyptian strongholds and forces.

This time Samson won against the descendants of Delilah. Yitzhak Sadeh, first commander of the Palmach, headed a mechanized brigade that, mounted on jeeps, command cars, and sometimes on horses, bought from Bedouins, carried out their own attacks against the Egyptians. These fighters earned the name "the animals of the Negev."

As it was in Jerusalem, the feeling in the south and in the Negev was that this was a war of life or death. The Israelis went out to hit the Egyptians with everything they had. The Egyptians boasted a mighty fleet compared with the poorly equipped Israeli Navy, which had only recently come into being. It was impossible in one day to turn a fleet of phantom ships used to ferry immigrants to Palestine into a fighting armada. Thus when the Israelis sought to sink Egypt's flagship, the battleship *Emir Farouk,* the only way

Yitzhak Rabin (left) and Yigal Allon (right), architects of the Egyptian surrender in the Negev (below).

they could do this was by a naval commando raid.

A youngster by the name of Yohai Bin-Nun, who fought in the Palmach, set out on a small Italian dinghy loaded with dynamite to sink the royal battleship off the coast of Gaza. It was a sort of human torpedo, similar to those that Italian frogmen had successfully used in World War II against British battleships. On Friday, October 22, 1948, under cover of darkness, Yohai silently approached the 1,500-ton Egyptian warship. His orders were to jump off the boat about three hundred yards from the ship. But he wanted to ensure that his small craft would crash into the mighty battleship, so he remained on board until he had a mere seventy-five yards to spare. Still he managed to witness the dynamite-laden boat exploding as it crashed into the *Emir Farouk*. Within three minutes the great Egyptian battleship had overturned and sunk.

Yohai was awarded the Medal for Bravery for this action, one of only twelve fighters who were awarded this honor in the War of

Independence. Israelis have always been very stingy about decorating their heroes. Eight years later, Bin-Nun was appointed commander of the Israeli Navy.

The attack on the Egyptian flagship was carried out within the framework of a decision taken by Ben-Gurion and approved by the government to expel the Egyptians and chase them back to Egypt. Ben-Gurion himself described this move as "the toughest decision we were called on to make from the moment we decided on establishing the State." Thus it was Israel that initiated belligerent acts, violating the cease-fire imposed by the United Nations. Ben-Gurion wanted to exploit Israeli successes on the other fronts and gain control of the Negev to frustrate any chance for the U.N. plan detaching this vast desert from the State of Israel. Bernadotte's plan, following his assassination, had become something of a sacred testament. The pretext Ben-Gurion used was that the Egyptians themselves had violated the cease-fire agreement. They had, in fact, fired on Israeli convoys seeking to reach besieged Jewish settlements in the Negev.

The Israeli Army by this time had mobilized one hundred thousand men and women. Each day fresh shipments of arms arrived. Most importantly thousands of new immigrants arrived at the port of Haifa, the able-bodied among them being mobilized immediately and sent to the Negev and Galilee fronts.

To enable him to break through to the Negev and expel the Egyptians, Yigal Allon had two Palmach brigades placed under his command, in addition to the Givati Brigade and the "Old Man's" Brigade. The "Old Man" was Yitzhak Sadeh, founder of the Palmach and its first commander. Sadeh became one of those under the command of his pupil, Allon. He headed the Eighth Brigade, which was called the Israel Defense Force "armored brigade." These days, when Israel has thousands of tanks at its disposal and is con-

Ben-Gurion with, to his right, Yohai Bin-Nun, responsible for the destruction of the Emir Farouk, *flagship of the Egyptian navy.*

sidered one of the greatest experts on tank warfare, it seems ludicrous to think that this is the name they gave to that brigade. Sadeh had but a few armored cars available to him that carried infantrymen, three medium-sized tanks, and eight light tanks. But in the conditions prevailing at that stage, this force was regarded by the Israelis as large and impressive.

The operations officer on the Negev front was a young red-headed officer, Yitzhak Rabin. The Egyptians had their Third Division on Israel's southern flank blocking the way to the Negev and controlling vital key positions. The Egyptians attached to this division several semiregular Sudanese, Libyans, and the Muslim Brotherhood. These forces were deployed from south of Jerusalem through Beit Jubrin to a point north of Ashdod. They had also taken the Gaza Strip.

Allon promised Ben-Gurion he would defeat the Egyptians within seven days. The time factor was of extreme importance to Ben-Gurion, as he feared that the superpow-

The battle for the Negev: an Israeli aid station behind the front lines.

ers would intervene and put a stop to the fighting before Israel had managed to complete the campaign.

On October 15 Operation Yoav, designed to break the Egyptian siege in the Negev and create territorial continuity between this enormous desert region and the center of Israel, began. Among the objectives of the operation was also the capture of the Gaza Strip. The Egyptians dug into their positions and, with the support of artillery and planes, fought well. Already at that stage, the Israelis learned what would be revealed in future wars—that in defensive actions, the Egyptian position, the Israelis had to resort to face-to-face fighting.

One Egyptian stronghold (Hill 113) was not captured until some 250 Egyptian soldiers had fallen. Seven Israeli attacks on the Iraqi Sweidan police station, a huge and well-fortified police building at the entrance to the Negev, controlled by the Egyptians, failed. This fortress was eventually taken on November 9 by Sadeh himself.

Then the U.N. Security Council called for a cease-fire. Ben-Gurion was by this time ready to give up the idea of capturing the Gaza Strip—and indeed he eventually did give it up. The main thing was that the road to the Negev be opened.

Just then—five days after Allon's offensive started—the Israelis intercepted an Egyptian coded message that they had decided to withdraw to Gaza and Beersheba and sought the approval of their general headquarters in Cairo. This approval was given some four hours later, on the evening of October 20.

Allon now decided to concentrate all his efforts on the capture of Beersheba, the historical capital of the Negev, the city of Abraham according to Hebrew tradition. For this operation Allon sent in the Negev Brigade. The town at that time had about ten thousand residents, and its entire area stretched over a tract of land just 2.5 km long by 2 km wide. According to intelligence reports, there were four hundred Egyptian soldiers stationed in the town.

Palmach units, mounted on jeeps and command cars with a few armed personnel carriers (APC's), advanced on the town during the night and surprised its inhabitants at dawn. The Egyptians tried to blunt the attack with antitank and automatic fire. However, one Israeli company gained control of half the sand-swept city, and Egyptian soldiers began throwing up their hands in surrender. The commander of this company was a young, baby-faced Palmach officer, Avraham Adan, known by his nickname, "Bren." In time he would become one of the IDF's best-known tank commanders. In the 1973 Yom Kippur War, he would command the Armored Division, which helped encircle the Egyptian Third Army on the west side of the Suez Canal.

During the few days this campaign lasted, Ben-Gurion repeatedly visited command headquarters at the front. He wanted to be close to the scene of the action, to spur the commanders on by virtue of his very presence. Wishing to complete his offensive, he rejected pressures for a cease-fire called for by the Se-

Commanders of the Israeli Army.

curity Council. Ben-Gurion saw in the capture of Beersheba a very valuable military, political, and moral victory. "The capture of Beersheba," Ben-Gurion told Allon, "has enormous meaning. The Bible has given it worldwide prominence." Ben-Gurion ex-

David Ben-Gurion with his officers.

255

plained to Allon that for this reason it was essential that the town remain part of Israel. The way to the Negev was open.

Only then did Ben-Gurion agree to the U.N.'s cease-fire. He hurried to pay a visit to Beersheba, traveling in a convoy, arriving there after three of the vehicles became bogged down by floods. Allon's operation brought additional gains. Those Egyptians who had not managed to withdraw in time were squeezed into a narrow pocket in the region of Faluja. The Israelis encircled them, preventing the four thousand soldiers from escaping. The Egyptians stood up well to the conditions of siege. One of the officers caught in this pocket was a young major by the name of Gamal Abdel Nasser, a well-built, good-looking officer. He later took part in negotiations with Allon for the evacuation of the Egyptian soldiers.

Nasser would say much later that this experience had a profound influence on the whole course of his life. He accused the "rotten regime" in Egypt and the British, whom he greatly detested, for the Army's downfall. In 1952, it was this young major who, together with fellow officer Anwar al-Sadat, backed General Mohammed Naguib when he deposed King Farouk in a military coup and banished him from Egypt. They accused the King of a Palestine disaster, saying that he had sent them into battle ill-equipped, with faulty ammunition and an insufficient supply of weapons. Soon thereafter, Nasser became President of Egypt and himself failed in two wars waged against Israel.

Even before the war ended, Ben-Gurion carried out the final stage of his plans to wipe out any vestige of the days of the underground. Despite the successes of the Palmach in operations all over Eretz Yisrael—perhaps because of them—and even in the face of Yigal Allon's stunning victories and his own personal popularity, Ben-Gurion gave orders to disband the Palmach high command. In

Nasser besieged by the Israelis at Faluja.

this order Ben-Gurion decreed that the Palmach be dissolved and its brigades become an integral part of the Israeli Defense Force. At that time, the Palmach had its own high command, which Ben-Gurion, as Minister of Defense, was obliged to consult.

On this issue, a huge and bitter argument broke out between Ben-Gurion and the leaders of the Palmach. The Palmach commanders insisted that their commandos had made it possible for the IDF to be a special army—"a people's army." The insignia of the Palmach consisted of a sword and two sheaths of wheat, representing the art of war and cultivating the land.

Accordingly, they felt they ought to continue serving as an influence on the army as a whole, so the Palmach's commanders argued that the high command and its brigades be maintained in a special framework within the scope of the armed forces. They wanted to ensure that this force would in the future encourage the blend of fighters and settlers of the land—the combination of defense and kibbutzim.

But Ben-Gurion regarded the Palmach's continued existence as a private army, a danger he was not prepared to tolerate. He never equated the Palmach with the Irgun and the Stern Group, and there was no ground for such a comparison. But as a matter of principle, Ben-Gurion related to them on exactly the same basis. There would be no "special rights" groups in the IDF; there would be one, and only one, army.

There were those who even accused him of dissolving the Palmach high command in order to entrench his regime. They suggested Ben-Gurion did not want his political opponents in the other socialist parties, who held a majority in the ranks of the Palmach, to have such an outstanding fighting force at their disposal.

The battle for the Negev, 1948.

But Ben-Gurion was not put off by the enormous opposition and bitterness his decision evoked in the upper echelons of the

An Israeli army jeep in the Negev mountains.

The battle for the Negev: an Israeli attack against a village.

Palmach and within its ranks. They accepted his authority, although for many years afterward, they continued to point an accusing finger at Ben-Gurion and ask, "Why did you dissolve the Palmach?"

Now Ben-Gurion sought a way to take control of the whole of the Negev. Allon pressured him in this regard more than any other commander. Ben-Gurion's vision, as became plain in the course of the years, was of the need to make the desert bloom again and fill it with Jews in agricultural settlements. Indeed, when he resolved to go into the political wilderness in 1963, Ben-Gurion went to live in a small house on Kibbutz Sde Boker in the Negev.

At about the same time, Ben-Gurion renewed his contacts with King Abdullah, using as one of his emissaries Moshe Dayan. These contacts led to the signing of a secret armistice with Jordan. This agreement actually ensured the Jordanian King *de facto* annexation of the West Bank, Judea, and Samaria. Instead of a Palestinian Arab state being set up alongside the Jewish state, Jordan became the sovereign authority over the West Bank of Eretz Yisrael, as well as the Old City of Jerusalem. The Jordanian occupation continued for nineteen years, until June 1967.

Ben-Gurion then gave orders to mount an offensive to dislodge the Egyptian Army from its remaining points in the south. Once again,

An Israeli unit that has just seized an Egyptian flag, in the Sinai.

it was Yigal Allon who executed brilliant maneuvers and even carried the fight into enemy territory. He outflanked the Egyptian Army by sending his units to cut off their rear. Allon's units broke through into the Sinai Desert along the Abu Ageila–Al-Arish axis. This cut off the Army, which was encamped in the Gaza Strip. Allon got as far as the Al-Arish airfield and was about to take the town—the capital of northern Sinai—itself.

This was the first occasion on which the IDF captured territory outside the international boundaries of Israel. The wheel had turned full circle. The Egyptians called on the British for help, and London asked the United States to intervene. Both the British and

Americans sent ultimatums to Ben-Gurion, warning him to withdraw his troops from the Sinai Desert at once.

Allon gnashed his teeth on receiving this order from Ben-Gurion and tried to have it revoked. But eventually Allon withdrew from the Sinai before the Egyptians had surrendered. For the first time, Israeli Army commanders learned that they could not achieve a strategic gain on the battlefield. Because each time they were victorious, the superpowers would come to the aid of the Arabs.

Allon warned that this withdrawal would rule out the possibility of peace with Egypt. He was right, because this was only Israel's first withdrawal from Sinai. The Israelis

259

The dashing Ezer Weizman.

would retake the whole of Sinai again in the 1956 Suez campaign, only to pull back once more without having achieved peace. Later, in 1967, they would capture this area and again withdraw fifteen years later, in April 1982, at the time when a formal peace with Egypt was achieved.

But at least Allon's offensive produced a situation in which Israeli forces now controlled the borders of the Sinai Desert. The British tried to chase them from there, too. The first time they saw their Egyptian protégés on the receiving end of a beating, the British sent in aircraft to threaten the Israeli forces. Ben-Gurion was not deterred by the much-vaunted RAF. He sent out Israeli Air Force planes to meet them.

One of the pilots was Ezer Weizman, himself a daring ex-RAF pilot who flew the first Israeli Spitfire, a plane that had been assembled from various parts at Israeli workshops. The Israelis turned it into a reconnaissance plane. But its camera was an old one, so when Weizman went out to photograph Damascus in November 1948, so he later told me, he had to hover over the Syrian capital for more than two hours in order to photograph the whole city, going backward and forward over Damascus airport so the camera could photograph all the targets.

Now Weizman was one of four Israeli fighter pilots who went out to intercept the British planes. Four Israeli planes against twelve British ones fought an air battle over Al-Arish on January 7, 1949. The Israelis downed two British aircraft and on the same day brought down three more.

"My dream after that was to attack an

Egyptian Army train and an Egyptian battleship," Weizman later told me. "I realized one of those dreams. In the Suez campaign in 1956, I did in fact strafe an Egyptian train in the Sinai Desert."

After the severe blow they suffered in the air that day, the British stopped sending their planes to intervene on Egypt's behalf.

The following day—January 8, 1949—Ben-Gurion posed this question in his diary: "Did the war end today?" It did not. Eilat, Israel's southern harbor, had still to be captured.

Eilat

YIGAL ALLON'S contribution to the capture of Eilat was not confined only to his planning and commanding the operation. His nonstop pressure on Ben-Gurion to proceed with the campaign was an equally vital factor. The original Partition Plan had incorporated the Negev into the territory of the state, but the Israelis, who had settled only the northern part of this barren desert, hardly maintained any presence there. The Bernadotte Plan gave the British and the Jordanians—as well as the Egyptians—the hope that the Negev would be given to the Arabs. King Abdullah hoped to annex the Negev and so deployed units of his Arab Legion at various points throughout the desert. The Jordanians controlled the Gulf of Eilat and patrolled the southern Negev in jeeps and on camels; negotiating existing roads through the desert to Eilat with vehicles was extremely difficult.

Ben-Gurion had been busy conducting renewed secret contacts with Abdullah and the signing of an armistice with Jordan. He now turned his attention to negotiating a similar agreement with Egypt. The general feeling was that the War of Independence had ended without Israel being in control of the Negev and Eilat.

Ben-Gurion sent Moshe Dayan to hold secret talks with Abdullah. The Jordanian monarch angrily tried putting the blame for the war on Golda Meir. "She could have prevented the war," he complained. When he heard she had been appointed Israel's first ambassador to Moscow, his cynical rejoinder was: "Very good—keep her there!"

Allon urged the general staff to capture Eilat, which was not then the thriving port city and holiday resort it is today. Known then as Um Rashrash, it was merely a point on the map, with a one-story clay police station.

Since Ben-Gurion did not want any disruptions in the negotiations he was conducting with the Jordanians and Egyptians, he directed Allon to "refrain from engaging in

The capture of Eilat on March 10, 1949: the Israeli flag is hoisted.

262

Golda Meir, ambassador to the Soviet Union in 1948. King Abdullah exclaimed, "Excellent! Leave her there," upon receiving the news of her appointment.

combat in this campaign." In other words, the Negev and Eilat had to be taken without a battle.

Reconnaissance teams set out for Eilat to check the indirect routes leading there. They also discovered a natural airfield—a wide flatland in the heart of the desert. Allon dispatched two brigades to Eilat under the command of Nahum Sarig and Nahum Golan,

two first-class officers who had seen a great deal of combat during the War of Independence. The two brigades advanced through the desert in a pincer movement. Despite Ben-Gurion's order, when Allon's soldiers were called on to open fire, they did.

Units of the Jordanian Army, fearing a trap, withdrew across the border to Jordan. The appearance of the two sizable Israeli

forces on makeshift roads stunned Abdullah's men. Aside from sporadic bursts of fire from their outposts in the desert, they did not try to interfere. As they overcame natural obstacles and advanced over extremely dangerous ground, a race developed between the two Israeli brigades over who would be the first to reach the southernmost point of the state.

Sarig entrusted an improvised Israeli flag to Avraham Adan, one of his company commanders. It was a piece of white cloth on which the Star of David had been painted in blue ink. "You must be the first to reach Eilat," Sarig ordered.

Adan's company was indeed the first to see the sparkling blue waters of the Gulf of Eilat, traveling part of the route in command cars, and part on foot under the scorching desert sun. When they neared the police station, they were surprised to find it totally empty. Eilat was taken without a shot being fired. The Legion had been ordered to withdraw to the nearby Jordanian port of Aqaba.

The Israelis rushed to the flagpole in front

of the clay police station. Adan pulled out the sweat-soaked and dusty flag from his shirt. His friends held the pole, as he climbed up and unfurled the flag. It was four o'clock in the afternoon of March 10, 1949.

The unfurling of the "ink flag" in Eilat became one of the best-known photographs of the War of Independence, comparable to the raising of the United States flag on Iwo Jima in World War II, an act which symbolized the end of the war and the Israeli presence at the southernmost tip of their country. The moment the flag was flying over Eilat, the entire company stood at attention and sang the national anthem, "Hatikvah." Minutes later, an officer named Sashka yelled out, "I want to be the first Israeli to swim in the Gulf of Eilat." With only his army cap on his head, he dived into the crisp blue waters. Since that brief swim, tourists from around the world have come to know the clear and refreshing waters of the gulf of this important port city, which now boasts over twenty-two thousand inhabitants.

Yigal Allon sent an urgent cable to Ben-Gurion: "Delighted to inform you that our forces completed the operation, including the liberation of the Israeli Gulf of Eilat [Gulf of Aqaba]. The Israeli flag is now flying over the police station at Um Rashrash. The Army of the South is happy."

Ben-Gurion wrote in his diary: "This may be the greatest event of the last months, if not of the entire war. Not one drop of blood spilled!"

In a private letter to Ben-Gurion, Allon now recommended that it was an appropriate time to expel Abdullah's Arab Legion from the West Bank, the heart of Eretz Yisrael.

"Abdullah's Hashemite Army remains our young state's most dangerous enemy," Allon

Capture of Eilat: Sashka is the first Israeli officer to swim in the waters of the gulf.

267

wrote, warning that if Israel were to accept "the Hashemite invader's continued presence in parts of Eretz Yisrael, this would amount to a *de facto* recognition on our part of the political annexation of these territories to the Kingdom of Transjordan." Allon, the brilliant strategist, added that the Jordan River was the "most secure and natural border of the entire country."

Yigal Allon (center), following the capture of Eilat.

Ben-Gurion, however, had had enough of war. He was willing to sign a peace treaty with the Arabs based on the borders the Israelis had demarcated on the battlefield. Ben-Gurion believed Abdullah's promise that he would guarantee Jewish access to the Western Wall in the Old City of Jerusalem.

He felt deeply that it was time to break out of the cycle of hostilities. The first democratic elections were held in the State of Israel on January 25, 1949, making Israel the only democracy in the Middle East—a situation that applies to this very day. Ben-Gurion's party received forty-six of the one hundred twenty

seats in the first Knesset. Herut, the party of his arch-rival Begin, received only fourteen.

Ben-Gurion was already occupied with the absorption of the new immigrants. Some 150,000 had arrived since May 15, 1948. "The fate of the state depends on immigration," said Ben-Gurion. "We have indeed made conquests, but without settling Israel, conquests are of no decisive importance—not in the Negev, not in Galilee, and not in Jerusalem. Settling the country—this is the real conquest." Ben-Gurion thus rejected Allon's proposal to drive King Abdullah's army from the West Bank.

In retrospect there is no doubt that had Allon not been the commander of the Southern Front, the Negev and Eilat might never have been included in the territory of the State of Israel. More than any other commander during that war, Allon influenced the fixing of the borders of the state. "He was the best general we had," his operations officer, Yitzhak Rabin, told me.

Allon left the Army to become one of Israel's most prominent political leaders. He had been proven right in his strategic evaluations. What Allon proposed to do in 1949 was ultimately carried out in 1967 by his pupil, Yitzhak Rabin, who had then become the IDF chief of staff, when he pushed King Hussein's Arab Legion out of Judea, Samaria, and Jerusalem, and ousted the Egyptians from the Gaza Strip.

I recently asked Rabin, now Israel's Defense Minister, how he and the men of his generation had succeeded in accomplishing what they had in 1948–49. His answer was brief and low-keyed: "We had faith, and we simply believed."

Hope

Hatikvah

AT THE END of the War of Independence, after sixteen months of bloodshed that left six thousand Jews, both soldiers and civilians, dead, and sixteen thousand wounded, the guns fell silent. Most Israelis were convinced that peace with the Arab states was at hand. They had, after all, been victorious on the battlefield. The Arab armies had been thrown back behind the international borders, except for the Arab Legion, which remained in control of the Old City and the West Bank, and the Egyptian Army, which had taken the Gaza Strip.

The Israelis, exhausted by the long war and not yet fully comprehending the magnitude of the Holocaust, believed that the armistice agreements signed with Jordan, Egypt, Syria, and Lebanon would lead to peace treaties, enabling them to begin healing their wounds and building their country. And in 1949 Israel was closer to real peace than at any time since. Israeli officers met with their Egyptian, Jordanian, and Syrian counterparts in the bilateral armistice committees, in a friendly at-

Eastern European immigrants arriving in Haifa in 1948.

mosphere dealing with ongoing problems along the borders. Ben-Gurion continued his secret contacts with King Abdullah.

For us, the generation of Israelis who take the State of Israel for granted, and particularly the ensuing generations born into an existing State of Israel, the heroes of the War of Independence became a symbol, a shining example to be emulated in all areas: settlement, defense, and the absorption of millions of immigrants who came to Israel.

The saga of the *Exodus* and the daring op-

A stroll in Tel Aviv.

A new wave of immigrants arriving at a camp.

The Shaar Aliyah center near Haifa, 1950: the newly arrived immigrants claim their baggage (below) and set up their first camp.

274

Recently arrived immigrants in the camp of St. Luke near Jerusalem,
1948.

A woman fighter from the Haganah with the Israeli flag.

erations of the Haganah and Irgun, are all part of our national heritage—the struggle of the few against the many. The memory of the Arab armies' attack on the still unborn state is indelibly inscribed on our minds. It was reinforced twenty-five years later by the bitter memory of the Syrian and Egyptian armies' surprise onslaught on Yom Kippur in 1973. If one adds to this the horrors of the Holocaust, which every Israeli knows from those who barely survived that hell on earth, one realizes the unusually heavy heritage that each and every Israeli carries with him.

In their wildest imagination, Ben-Gurion and his contemporaries could not have dreamed that Israel would have to go to war so many times in a space of nearly forty years following the creation of the State.

To their consternation, the Israelis over the years have discovered that the Arabs were not willing to accept the State of Israel as a fact of life. In most of the wars and in the various skirmishes between them, Israel has won stunning victories.

There has been peace with Egypt, in practice, for some ten years now. The opportunity to resolve the conflict between two nations, the Jews and Arabs, has finally arrived. The true partners to the conflict, however, live on the two sides of the Jordan River. King Hus-

Planting trees in the village of Shaar Aliyah, 1948.

sein rules the East Bank of Eretz Yisrael, called the Hashemite Kingdom of Jordan, and Israel controls the West Bank of Eretz Yisrael, the area west of the Jordan River. The territories of Judea and Samaria, as well as the Gaza Strip, now in the hands of Israel, are the core of the conflict. Hundreds of thousands of Arabs, as well as a few thousand Jews who have built over one hundred settlements, live in these areas. After the War of Independence, after the forty-year war of liberation that the Israelis have been forced to conduct on their soil, with a united Jerusalem as their capital, the primary task still lies ahead of them: how to coax the Palestinians into a path leading to the establishment of a joint Israeli-Palestinian federation or confederation on both sides of the Jordan River.

Whoever leads the way toward this goal holds the key to peace between the two peoples. It is said that this is "impossible," "not feasible," "unthinkable." These, however, were the very words used to describe the establishment of the State of Israel, now celebrating its fortieth anniversary.

Significant Dates in the Birth of Israel

Date	The Land of Israel	In the World
1839	Jewish community numbers 12,000 souls.	Ottoman Empire rules over Palestine.
1860		Birth of Theodor Herzl in Budapest.
1870	Creation of the first Jewish School of Agriculture in Mikveh Israel.	
1878	Creation of Petah-Tikvah, the first village for agricultural settlement.	
1886	Arab attacks against Jewish communities in Palestine.	
1888	Start of the First Aliyah (wave of immigration).	
1895		In France, Alfred Dreyfus is demoted from the rank of captain.
1896		Herzl publishes *The Jewish State (Der Judenstaat)*.
1897		Herzl establishes the first Zionist Congress in Basel.
1898	Herzl spends October–November in Palestine.	
1904	Start of the Second Aliyah.	Death of Theodor Herzl.
1904/ 1905		Pogroms against the Jews in Russia.
1909	Establishment of Degania, the first cooperative community, and of Tel Aviv, the first Jewish town.	
1914		Turkey allies itself with Germany in World War I.
1917	The British, victorious in Judea and Jerusalem, establish martial law in Palestine.	Balfour declaration concerning the Jewish National Homeland.
1918	Jewish battalions enter Palestine, conquer Samaria and Galilee.	
1920	Britain receives the League of Nations' mandate for Palestine and sets up an Arab government in Transjordan, which is split off from Palestine. Start Third Aliyah. Hebrew recognized as official language. Arabs commit outrages against Jews in Jerusalem: Zev Jabotinsky openly organizes a defense force; he is arrested by the British. Creation of the Haganah in Jerusalem.	World War I allied victors hold a conference in San Remo.
1921	Arab outrages continue.	
1922	First population census in Palestine: 83,790 Jews; 590,890 Muslims; 73,024 Christians.	SDN ratifies the British Mandate (July 24). London establishes the Emirate of Transjordan in the eastern part of Palestinian territory.
1929	Jews of Hebron and Safed massacred by Arabs. Creation of Jewish Agency.	

Date	The Land of Israel	In the World
1931	Split in Haganah and creation of the Irgun.	
1933	Jews continue to settle. Arrival of 30,000 Jews.	Hitler comes to power in Germany. Jews start leaving Germany and other parts of Europe to settle in Palestine.
1934	The *Velos* arrives with the first 350 illigal immigrants. Arrival of 42,000 Jews.	
1935	Arrival of 62,000 Jews.	Proclamation of the Nuremberg Laws.
1936	Arab uprisings; outrages against the Jews. Intervention of the Haganah. Irgun reprisals against Arab terrorists.	
1937	Implantation of "tower and enclosure" communities in the Jordan and Bet Shean valleys. Arab outrages. The Haganah trains its officers.	In Britain, the Peel Commission recommends the partition of Palestine.
1938	Haganah trains paramilitary units with British help. Jews consolidate their settlements in Galilee by creating Hanita.	Munich agreement.
1939	Arab revolt kept in check. Publication of the White Paper in Britain, which limits both Jewish immigration and the purchase of land by Jews.	Outbreak of World War II.
1940	Haganah creates its first air unit. Jewish volunteers join the British Army. Avraham Stern (Yair) creates the Lehi, or Stern Group.	News of Nazi brutality against Jews begins to filter through.
1941/ 1942	Haganah creates the Palmach to fight the Germans.	A Vichy regime in Syria. Rommel's troops advance on Egypt. Germany invades the Soviet Union.
1942	News filters through of the death camps. The British assassinate "Yair" Stern in Tel Aviv.	Rommel arrives at El Alamein.
1943		Uprising of the Warsaw ghetto.
1944	Stern group assassinates Lord Moyne in Cairo. Haganah denounces as terrorists the Lehi and Irgun and hands them over to the British. Irgun proclaims "a rebellion against the occupying British."	Allied landings in Normandy.
1945	Haganah resume illegal immigration. Mosad Aliyah Bet puts together a flotilla of 65 boats, which will transport another 85,000 refugees to Palestine until May 15, 1948.	Surrender of the Third Reich. Jews discover that the Nazis have massacred a third of their people, six million. Election victory for the British Labour Party.
1946	The Haganah, Irgun, and Lehi, having founded the "Insurrection Movement" in October 1945, attack British targets in Palestine. The British decide to send members of the Irgun and Stern groups to the gallows.

June 29:
"Black Sabbath"—the British arrest the leaders of the Haganah and discover their arms cache.
July 22:
The Irgun blow up the British headquarters at the King David Hotel, Jerusalem. Members of Irgun and Lehi are exiled to Africa.

October 6:
In one fell swoop, the Haganah establishes 11 communities in the southern Negev to ensure future control of the Negev. | Trial of war criminals at Nuremburg. The British send illegal Jewish immigrants into Cyprus from Palestine.

London takes considerable steps to "get rid of Terrorism (Jewish) in Palestine." |

Date	The Land of Israel	In the World
1947	The Haganah increases its arms purchases in Europe.	Secret Haganah centers operate in France, Italy, and Switzerland.
	May: The Irgun storm the prison of Acre, dubbed the "British Bastille."	At the U.N., Soviet representative Andrei Gromyko supports the rights of the Jews to a state.
	July: The 4,515 passengers on the *Exodus* are arrested by the British and sent back to Port-de-Bouc.	The U.N. sends a special commission to Palestine.
	September 9: The *Exodus* refugees are brought back to Hamburg and unloaded by force.	The U.N. commission recommends the partition of Palestine.
	November: Golda Meir and King Abdullah meet secretly.	
1947	November 29: Zionist leaders accept the Partition Plan—the Arabs reject it.	November 29: The U.N. General Assembly, supported by the U.S. and the U.S.S.R., adopts the Partition Plan for Palestine. People and finances are mobilized throughout the Jewish communities in the world, especially in the U.S.
	November 30: Arab attacks committed in Jerusalem, Tel Aviv, and on the roads. Ben-Gurion mobilizes the population and the fighting units of the Haganah.	
1948	January: First Syrian advances into Upper Galilee.	The Haganah negotiate the purchase of arms from Czechoslovakia. "Cold War" begins between U.S. and U.S.S.R.
	February: Invasion by the "Palestinian Liberation Army" in the center of the country—2 explosives claim dozens of victims in Jerusalem. The noose around Jerusalem tightens.	
	March: Secret landing of the first planeload of weapons from Prague, and the start of the airlift to equip the fighters of the Haganah and the Israeli Defense Forces.	Jewish and non-Jewish pilots throughout the world volunteer to help the young state.
	April: Fighting breaks out in the effort to open the road to Jerusalem.	
	April 9: Units from the Irgun and Lehi attack the Arab village of Deir Yassin—there are women among the victims.	The *Lino*, loaded with arms for the Arabs, is sunk by the Haganah in Italy.
	April 14: Arabs massacre a convoy of doctors and nurses on the road to Mount Scopus.	
	April 21: After fierce fighting, Haifa falls to the Jews. The Arabs flee.	
	May 10: Last effort for peace; Golda Meir and King Abdullah meet secretly in Amman.	
	May 12: Ben-Gurion's proposal that independence be proclaimed is accepted with a majority vote by the National Council.	U.S. pushes for a delay in the creation of the State of Israel to allow the U.N. to obtain a cease-fire.
	May 13: Jaffa is taken—Arabs continue to flee.	

May 14:
The Arab Legion seizes Gush Etzion. At four P.M., in the city of Tel Aviv, Ben-Gurion proclaims the independence of Israel.

Hundreds of thousands of Jews organize to leave for Israel.

May 15:
Arab armies invade Israel. The Egyptian Air Force bombs Tel Aviv. Syrian and Iraqi offensive in the valley of the Jordan.

U.S. recognizes the State of Israel.

May 28:
Arab Legion conquers the Jewish Quarter in the Old City of Jerusalem. The Latrun attack to break through the siege of Jerusalem fails. Ben-Gurion proclaims the creation of the Israeli Defense Force, which replaces the Haganah.

June:
The Burma Road is opened, breaking the siege of Jerusalem.

U.N. imposes the first truce.

June 22:
Atalena, the Irgun's ship, is sunk off Tel Aviv by the Haganah. Civil war is avoided. The Irgun is dismantled.

End of June:
Definitive departure of the British.

July 11:
Ramle and Lod are taken; Arab inhabitants flee.

July 15:
Israeli Air Force bombs Cairo for the first time.

July 16:
Nazareth falls to the Israelis.

September:
U.N. mediator Folke Bernadotte proposes to cut Negev from Israeli territory.

September 17:
Stern Group assassinates Bernadotte in Jerusalem. Ben-Gurion orders the arrest of Stern members and dismantling of the organization.

Angry reactions against the young State of Israel.

October 15:
Israeli offensive to push Egyptian Army out of the south. Fall of Beersheba. Egyptian troops encircled in the Faluja pocket.

London continues to help Amman and Cairo.

October 22:
Egyptian flagship *Emir Farouk* is sunk by Yohai Bin-Nun. Israeli Army mops up in Galilee. Defeat of the Arab Redemption Army.

December:
First breakthrough of the Israeli Army into the Sinai.

Washington demands immediate withdrawal of Israeli troops.

| 1948 | Arrival of 120,000 immigrants despite the war. | |

| 1949 | January:
Egyptian Army defeated. First legislative elections in Israel: Knesset established.

February:
Armistice agreement signed with Egypt. | |

March:
Eilat and the Negev are captured. End of the War of Independence.

Negotiations with Lebanon, Transjordan, and Syria lead to an armistice.

The photographs in this book are from:
A.F.P.: p. 10–11
Archives Paris Match: pp. 19, 33, 75, 77, 81, 128, 129, 154–155.
Associated Press: pp. 115, 118–119, 128, 129.
Robert Capa, Magnum: pp. 144–145, 146–147, 184–185, 188, 195, 210, 220, 224, 270, 271, 272, 273, 275.
René Dazy: p. 31.
Keystone: pp. 32, 33, 54–55, 60–61, 96, 98–99, 106–107, 115, 116, 120, 130–131, 132–133, 209, 246, 247, 248, 252, 256.
United Press: pp. 86–87, 108–109, 176.
Rights reserved: pp. 17, 44, 45, 105, 262–263.

The author also wishes to thank: The archives of the Israeli Defense Forces; the Jabotinsky Institute, Israel; Beit Yair, in the name of Abraham Stern; the Israeli Government Press Office; the Museum of the Israeli Defense Forces; Beit Haganah; *Bamahane,* the journal of the Israeli Army; Moshe Eitan.

Further thanks are due to Sol Lester for his document on (p. 74) and for photograph (p. 76), and to Hans Pinn (Exodus), as well as to all the anonymous photographers without whose contributions many parts of this history would not have been possible.

ABOUT THE AUTHOR

URI DAN is the author and co-author of over a dozen books that have been published internationally, including *Ninety Minutes at Entebbe*, *The Mossad*, and *Blood Libel: The Inside Story of General Ariel Sharon's History-Making Suit Against Time Magazine*. His career as a journalist spans over three decades of Israeli history. Reporting from the heat of the battlefronts, Mr. Dan wrote for Israel's largest daily newspaper, *Maariv*, from 1957–1981, serving as Military and Defense Correspondent, as Correspondent in Western Europe, and ultimately, as Chief of Correspondents. In 1982, Mr. Dan became Media Adviser to Defense Minister Ariel Sharon, and accompanied him throughout the War in Lebanon.

Special journalistic assignments have taken him, over the years, to the United States, the Soviet Union, Vietnam, and South America. He is winner of the Overseas Press Club of America prize for Best Magazine Interpretation of Foreign Affairs.

Mr. Dan is currently the Mideast Correspondent for the *New York Post*. He lives in Tel Aviv with his wife and son.

YOSSI HAREL was Commander of the ship *Exodus* when it made its historic 1947 journey to Palestine. He has provided his compelling first-hand account of that time in the *Exodus* Chapter of this book.